# MATCH
## OF MY LIFE

T0159567

# MATCH
# OF MY LIFE

Twelve stars relive their greatest games

# Wolves

## Simon Lowe

This edition first published by Pitch Publishing 2012

Pitch Publishing
A2 Yeoman Gate
Yeoman Way
Durrington
BN13 3QZ
www.pitchpublishing.co.uk

A CIP catalogue record is available for this book
from the British Library

ISBN 978-1-9080517-5-2

Typesetting and origination by Pitch Publishing.

Printed by Nutech Print Services - India

# Acknowledgements

Thanks to John Hendley, Graham Hughes, Mark Eagle, and Peter Pridmore at Wolverhampton Wanderers Football Club. Their help has been invaluable in the preparation and promotion of the book.

Of course thanks go to each of the 12 former players who took part in this book. Each and every one greeted me with open arms and several cups of coffee. Not to mention, of course, a wealth of anecdotes, stories and memories which form the chapters on the pages of this book.

But the biggest thanks must go to Peter Creed, the honorary secretary of the Wolves Former Players Association. Without his persuasive and organisational powers, this book would not have been possible. Thanks, Peter.

*Simon Lowe*

*Dedicated to Peter Broadbent*

# Contents

# Introduction

THERE IS NO greater pleasure than whiling away hours in the company of great footballers who are keen to recount a wealth of fabulous stories about their careers. To talk to the likes of Steve Bull, Bert Williams, John Richards and Ron Flowers provides the listener with a wealth of experience of 60 years of football played at the highest level. I found it fabulously rewarding in many different ways, not least because, often, meeting heroes can be an experience best played out in the imagination rather than in reality. Without exception the dozen Wolves legends I met gave of themselves as I interviewed them in the same way that they gave to their loyal supporters during their Molineux careers.

Each of the players featured in this book shared with me their ups and downs in a lifetime of football and it was wonderful to relive each of these great achievements with them. Now I hope that this book allows them to share their recollections of those wonderful matches, glorious victories and personal gallantry with you. Their success whilst wearing the famous Old Gold and Black connects these men and ensures the continuing affection of Wolves supporters of all ages, even, in some cases, over 50 years after the event.

But the most striking aspect of the connection between these 12 heroes that I discovered during the process of conducting the interviews which form this book, is the immense strength of character and purpose which they share. No matter that they played with such distinction for Wolves over a number of eras spanning more than half a century. It struck me immediately that they shared the inner belief which makes any person successful. They oozed pride, passion and courage, while, at the same time, discussing their achievements with a humility that only the truly great possess and which we mere mortals must stand in awe and wonder at.

But it was only as I chatted to all 12 of the players that I realised that each had been successful not only once in life, as a footballer for which they are naturally best remembered, but twice. Bert Williams, for example became a hugely successful property developer, Roy Swinbourne made his way by selling tyres, Malcolm Finlayson still owns a steel wholesalers in Kingswinford, Ron Flowers still has his sports shop right in the middle of Wolverhampton itself and Derek Parkin has only recently retired from his successful post-football career as a landscape gardener.

No matter what their choice of career after football, the quality which binds these great players together remains the same as that which saw them become such a success and, as a consequence, such household names at the Wolves. Namely the desire to make the most of their talent. It takes something special to succeed in the brash and unforgiving world of professional football, but to then become a success in another line of work shows how remarkable these men are. Talent in itself is not enough to ensure the kind of legendary status reached by all 12 of the participants in this book. There has to be more to such meteoric success than that and the unquantifiable special something - Simon Cowell's *X Factor* if you like - is clearly present in each of these men simply as human beings as much as anything else.

While, naturally, modern supporters will be far more concerned about Wanderers returning to the top flight of English football and staying there, I hope Wolves fans feel the warm glow of glories past coming through the pages of this book. It has been a privilege to compile it for you.

*Simon Lowe*

# Foreword

## by Sir Jack Hayward

OBVIOUSLY MY MOST memorable match to date was the play-off final at Cardiff on 26th May 2003, when we beat Sheffield United 3-0 to go into the Premier League. I didn't have a decent night's sleep for the previous two weeks and even at half-time I was still nervous. I think the defining moment was when Matt Murray saved their penalty just after the start of the second half. What a day! What a night!

The 3-2 win over Newcastle in the third round of the FA Cup on 5th January 2003 was another great day. George Ndah scored what proved to be the winner in the 49th minute following a breathtaking run, after Newcastle had nullified our 2-0 lead.

The 4-3 victory over Leicester in the Premier League on 25th October 2003, when we were 3-0 down at half-time, was also very memorable - Colin Cameron scoring twice (one a penalty), then another from Alex Rae and the winning goal by Henri Camara in the 86th minute. It was difficult to make intelligent conversation to the visiting directors both at half-time and full time!

What about the penalty shoot-out against Sheffield Wednesday in the FA Cup fourth round replay at Molineux on 8th February 1995? I remember Andy Thompson taking the first kick and missing for the first time ever that I can recall – and Robbie Dennison also failed from the spot. I really didn't know what was happening after that and I asked my son to explain. He yelled at me "It's sudden death, Dad, for God's sake, it's sudden death!!" Paul Jones was our hero, saving from Chris Waddle and then Don Goodman's successful kick gave us victory in an amazing heartstopping tense shoot-out.

At the time, Don was staying at the Mount Hotel in Wolverhampton with his wife and children, as were my wife and myself. At breakfast the next morning I congratulated him and asked if he was nervous before taking the kick. He replied that he wasn't, because he didn't know what was going on either and certainly didn't realize that it all depended on him!?

Thinking of that match, I like the true story of the Wolves fan who left the Stadium when we were 3-1 down in the penalty shoot-out. When he got home to Penn, his next-door neighbour was still up despite the late hour and said to the Wolves fan, "so we won!" To which the fan replied, "No, we lost on penalties." "But", said the neighbour, "I heard the roar of the crowd, so I know we've won!" I wonder how far it is from Molineux to Penn as the crow flies or as the Molineux Roar carries?

I have carried on too far. Read on for the real memories.

BERT WILLIAMS: BORN 31 JANUARY 1922, BILSTON; 420 GAMES, 0 GOALS

# Bert Williams

## Wolves 1 Manchester United 0

## FA Cup semi-final replay

## Saturday 2 April 1949

THERE'S NO FEELING on earth like it, coming out at Wembley. The Wolves' maximum gate was 50,000. There were double that there for the 1949 FA Cup Final. Everyone is out to enjoy it and they were all buzzing. Sammy Smyth scored a wonderful goal and Jesse Pye's first was a typical Wolves goal. Hancocks down the wing and a near post cross for Pye to head in. A good goal, scored from a quick attack of good, accurate passing.

But if you're asking me for games that stand out in my memory, I actually wouldn't pick that match. I'd probably would have to give you a couple that I'm still trying to forget. Losing 1-0 to the USA in the World Cup for a start! But I would actually select the FA Cup semi-final of 1949, when we played Manchester United, as my favourite match, or two matches in fact. And the reason is that it involved all the lads really, because it was such a fantastic team effort.

The spirit at the Wolves was unbelievable. Everybody was close friends, we knew each other intimately. We trained together, laughed together, joked together. If someone was having a bad match we would pull together and help him through. I don't ever remember playing in a Wolves match at which supporters left before the final whistle. They always believed that we could score to win a game or retrieve a situation, even if we were three down, because we believed it. And often we did it.

The idea of playing five forwards in those days was an admission that you wanted to score goals; that you wanted to win the game by attacking. We experienced defensive mentality and tactics first when I was playing for England in that defeat by the USA in the 1950 World Cup. I realised then that football was changing. Teams were going out to stop goals, rather than to score more than the opposition. But at Wolves we always strove to win. OK, we lost some games. But we only lost them trying to win.

I WAS ACTUALLY a West Brom fan when I was young. I used to go with my Dad in the local coach to the games at the Hawthorns to watch players like Billy Richardson and Harold Pearson. But the first goalkeeper I admired was Harry Hibbs. He was at Birmingham and I was a bit like him. He was small and quite agile. I only ever saw him play once, but I used to read about him in the paper all the time. Harry ended up being my manager at Walsall and it was he who sold me to the Wolves.

I am only 5ft 9in tall, which is small for a goalkeeper. My father, Walter, played in goal and he was a big influence on me. He taught me to keep my eye on the ball and get my body behind the ball. To do that properly you have to be superbly fit. And I have always had that as my aim in life. I never looked on training as work, but as an enjoyable exercise. I found that my fitness made me agile enough to be able to get across and save shots that I wouldn't be expected to save. What's important is how you read the game and your anticipation. Not simply your height.

My father was instrumental in getting me my first real chance in football. I played for a Bilston representative team after I left school at 14 and worked in a local factory, called Thompson's, where I also played in the works team at 15. A year later I got home from work one night and there at home was a man there called Andy Wilson, who was then manager of Walsall. He'd been a Scottish international. I spoke to him along with my Dad. It was a Friday night and Mr Wilson asked me if I wanted to sign and play the next day – at the Hawthorns against West Bromwich, who happened to be my team. I jumped at the opportunity. I'm pretty sure my Dad had something to do with the whole thing. The next day I went down to the ground to get on the coach to go to West Bromwich and the chap by the bus asked me, "What do you want, sonny?" And I said, "Oh, I'm playing today." I don't think he really believed me!

I GOT INTO the first team during the war, but then was away serving in the RAF for six years and everything came to a halt, of course. While I was stationed at Uxbridge and Tangmere, I guested for Chelsea and Nottingham Forest. Later on I was posted in Shropshire and Lincolnshire. But when the war was over I returned to Walsall knowing that several clubs were interested in signing me. Wolves agreed a fee with Walsall and I decided to join a more local club rather than move to one further away and I never regretted that decision once.

During my time as a physical training instructor in the war, I'd enjoyed the training aspect of keeping men fit. That's why Joe Gardiner, the Wolves coach, paid me the compliment of letting me train by myself. He knew that my exercises were vastly different to those for the outfield players; stretching and twisting and turning and sprinting. I know these days the lads have lovely physiques honed on indoor training with weights, but surely weight training shortens your muscles. It should be stretching that goalkeepers do. There's also no point sending a goalkeeper out on a ten mile run. It's more important to get your angles right. Learn to protect the near post and then anticipate the shot to the far.

Even though I was small I didn't get clobbered too often. Some centre-forwards, like Jackie Milburn, were gentlemen and didn't clatter into goalkeepers, however, there were some players who were a bit more rough, which was allowed then. Cullis wouldn't let me throw the ball out to a full-back. I had to kick it up to one of the wingers. But this wasn't simple long ball stuff - as we got accused of playing many a time. In order for it to work, my kicks had to be accurate and into the space that the wingers were about to run into and fight for the ball. There is a vast difference between hitting long balls accurately and simply whacking it upfield aimlessly. Jimmy Mullen was fast and Stan would not let him come back into our half, so you knew you could hit a ball out to the left and he would chase it down the wing.

The only time I ever wore gloves in football was on wet days, because the ball got very slippery. When I'd joined the RAF they gave me two boots, two pairs of socks, two suits and two pairs of gloves. I wore those gloves for keeping goal for a long time. Today the gloves they wear are like cow's udders, aren't they? I mean, they take away a lot of the basic skill. You know, if you turn your back and listen to them catching a ball you can tell if they are catching it properly. It sounds different. It's soft, rather than a hard slap, because you catch it with your fingers up and your thumbs behind the back of the ball. Not with your palms as there is more of a chance it will bounce out. Lower down you catch it with your elbows in and you body behind the ball. If you don't, every so often one will slip through and embarrass you. Having said that I do think it's more difficult to play today because of the light ball which swerves all over the place. That must be very difficult.

You need to be able to move your feet very quickly to get into the right place to take into consideration a last minute swerve or dip of the ball.

WOLVES HAD SUCH a good side after the war. Someone who didn't get enough credit was Major Buckley, the manager before and during the war. At the beginning of the conflict he fielded a team of virtually 16 or 17-year-olds, which meant by the end of the war the club had the nucleus of the 1939 FA Cup Final side, who were all experienced and all used to playing together, but also all these young players such as Billy Wright, Lol Kelly, Roy Pritchard, Billy Crook and Dennis Wilshaw who were coming through and were also now experienced, albeit in wartime football. Ted Vizard, after he took over as manager from Buckley in 1944, did not have to rebuild the side after the war. He bought myself, Johnny Hancocks and Jesse Pye, but the nucleus was there already.

That was a very different strategy to some other clubs. Sunderland, for example, used to buy their players. They paid big money for Len Shackleton, Billy Elliott from Bolton, winger Billy Bingham from Luton, Trevor Ford from Aston Villa and the two full-backs, plus Ray Daniel, the centre-half, from Arsenal. That's half the team isn't it? They were buying players in their prime, well after they'd been developed. They were known as the Bank of England club back then. Wolves preferred to develop their players and I think it paid dividends over quite a long period of time.

You have to remember that in 1949 United and Wolves were probably two of the best teams in the world. And we were drawn to play each other in the FA Cup semi-final up at Hillsborough. United were the cup holders having beaten Blackpool in the final the previous season.

But the reason we had to play quite so well and the reason this game stands out in my memory so much is that we played the majority of the match with injuries affecting the team. After just five minutes our left-back Roy Pritchard was injured in a collision with United's winger Delaney. Roy couldn't run properly and was forced to hobble around on the wing, while we reorganised the team.

Then after about an hour we picked up another injury. This time it was the other full-back, Lol Kelly, who was carried off on a stretcher following another accidental injury. I must stress that both injuries occurred in fair challenges. There was no sense of cheating or rough-housing on United's part. There was no malice in either challenge, they were just solid hard tackles. There wasn't really any nasty stuff at all. In those days you could go out and know players would go into the tackle behind the ball; none of this over the top stuff. You wouldn't get anyone rolling around either. You played according to those rules. Of course with no substitutes we effectively had nine men, even though Lol did reappear and played out on the other wing, hobbling even more badly than Roy!

So we had both full-backs injured and the United forward line was very dangerous. They had an England centre-forward in Jack Rowley, dashing wingers, much like ourselves, in Mitten and Delaney and crafty inside-forwards in Pearson and Morris; all internationals. We had to scrap and fight and battle to keep them out.

We'd actually managed to score our goal very early on. Allenby Chilton's short back pass was pounced upon by Jesse Pye, who raced through and squared to Sammy Smyth to score. United put enormous pressure on us then and had corner after corner. We dealt with the pressure fairly well, I think.

The headlines the next day mentioned Billy Wright. One even called him "the World's Greatest Player". I think this game brought him to national prominence. He was already well known, but on this occasion he marshalled our defence from his unusual new position of left-back, where he'd moved after Pritchard's injury. It seemed as if his blond head was rising above all the opposing players to nod the ball away and protect me.

Some people are captain because they can tell others what to do, but Billy always displayed his leadership by his actions on the pitch. He was 100% fit and gave 100 per cent effort. He wasn't even as tall as I am and yet he could get up well above opposing centre-forwards. He was a good man, a clean living man and an excellent person for anyone to copy going into sport. He was very down to earth. He couldn't understand what all the adoration was about and set an example by his efforts. He also stood out because of his blond hair. But primarily he stood out because he was a good player. If you had eleven Billy Wrights in your side you wouldn't go far wrong.

Alongside Bill was Bill Shorthouse. He was a straightforward, typical, do-it-as-it-should-be-done centre-half. He played hard, strong and was really good in the air. He nearly got an international cap. We were once playing at Liverpool and Mr Oakley, who was on the FA international selection committee, came into the dining room of the hotel before the game and said, "Lads, I've got news for you. There are three Wolverhampton players selected for England; Wright, Williams and Shorthouse." But when the team was actually announced on the Sunday the selectors had adjusted it for some reason. I don't know why and he never got in again.

I THINK THAT day the revamped defence did as much as it humanly could to protect me, but of course United did manage to break through occasionally. Only once did they beat me when a right wing cross found Charlie Mitten, their left-winger, running in at the far post to lob home as I flew out towards him. That goal arrived with around an hour to go, so we still had plenty of time to hold out, but we managed it by skill and luck. Then, of course, with it being a semi-final, we also had to play 30 minutes extra time. We kept United at bay throughout that period too, although I'm sure a few of our fans would have bitten their fingers to the quick!

Obviously I had a fair amount to do that day and enjoyed doing it and the result turned out very, very well for us. To have withstood over half a match playing with nine men against 11 was something else. That particular match epitomises everything the Wolves stood for in the game. 100 per cent. No prima donnas, giving everything they'd got. And Cullis demanded it. He would forgive anyone for trying, but he wouldn't forgive anyone who didn't. They wouldn't last long at Wolves. But I think that kind of spirit has gone from the game – and not just at Wolves.

In fact I think one of the things that has gone wrong with football is this short contract thing. I feel sorry for a manager who has built up his team, but the players decide that they want to go at the end of their contract. He has to start again. Back in my day you could not leave a club unless they said so. In fact you were always playing to be retained by the club. I remember that at the end of every season there always appeared on the noticeboard in the corridor at Molineux three lists of players; those who were retained, those who were open to transfer and those who were let go. That was how we found out whether we were to be retained or not.

Wages were fixed as well in those days, so we knew that a striker didn't get any more money than anyone else in the side. Everyone got the same. I think it's wrong that goalscorers earn so much more these days when it is just as important to create goals, or stop them, as to score them. And do you know, in all those years I never heard any complaint from a player about wages. In fact I am certain that all those great players at Wolves would have played for nothing. They loved to play to win and so many of them were local or developed by the club. Bill Shorthouse and I went to the same school. They had a good scouting system too. The chief scout, George Noakes, would get to hear about good local boys and sign them up as amateurs at 15. Then there was Wath Wanderers, the boys' team up in Yorkshire run by Mark Crook, the former Wolves player, where people like Roy Swinbourne and Ron Flowers came to prominence.

THE SEMI-FINAL replay was even more interesting as the two full-backs who had been injured weren't fit enough to play and we had to face United with two understudy full-backs in the team, one of whom, Alf Crook was making his first team debut and the other, Terry Springthorpe, hadn't played in the first team since September. But it gives you an idea of the strength of the Wolves squad in those days. Our reserve team was full of good players. These two came in and played very well. Springthorpe was an ideal physique for a full-back and had he not been at the Wolves he would have been a regular in anyone else's side.

It was another torrid battle between two very well-matched teams. I remember it rained heavily which made handling difficult and I think that played a part in the goal which won us the tie and put us through to Wembley. Despite plenty of chances at either end, both Bob Crompton and I were playing well, but with five minutes to go Jesse Pye cut in and shot. Crompton saved it once again, but the wet ball slipped from his grasp and allowed Sammy Smyth to pounce and head the ball into the net. We'd won.

SOMETIMES YOU DON'T know how well you've played until you read the papers. The next day they said nice things about me like, "The Wolves should strike a special medal for Bert Williams." Another paper declared, "Williams had a tremendous game with no thought for his own safety." It was nice to be acknowledged like that, but the most important thing was that Wolves had won. Not my own personal acclaim, but that the team had reached Wembley.

I remember one interesting thing from that game. I think when Sammy Smyth scored with just five minutes left everybody went and patted him on the back. That was quite a big expression of our delight as we'd nicked a goal right at the death of a semi-final which meant we were going to Wembley. But then Stan Cullis said afterwards, "You'll never do that again. I don't mind you shaking hands with him, but you'll never do that again." And what the manager said went. He could express his opinion and speak bluntly. But today if that happened the player would just say, "I'm off." It's the players that run the game these days isn't it? The tail's wagging the dog. It is really. It has gone a bit too far with all the advisors they have to run their lives. I didn't need a business manager on twelve quid a week I can tell you!

THAT SUMMER I won my first cap. I think playing in those high-profile games gave me a window for people to see more of me and make their decision to give me a chance. I'd played a couple of internationals during the war, but had never made it into the full squad until now. In those days there were at least half a dozen goalkeepers who could have played for England; Ditchburn, Fairbrother, Merrick to name a few. Frank Swift was definitely the best that I ever saw. He was big, but also agile, which is a rare combination.

Some years later I lost out unluckily too, so it swings both ways. I was selected to play for the Football League against the Scottish League and I got injured. So Gil Merrick came in and saved a penalty. Obviously you can't drop a player after a game like that. He kept me out for a long time after that. It did mean that I didn't play against Hungary when they tore

England apart in November 1953. I was substitute that day. I would have loved to have played in that game, though, against the best in the world. Gil and I had different styles. He would dive at balls from a standing position that I would move my feet to before flinging myself at pace, which I think allowed me to reach some balls I really shouldn't have. Gil also threw the ball out to Ramsey. He did that at Birmingham every week. He used the ball well. But because I didn't at Wolves, I think the England coach Walter Winterbottom preferred Gil's style.

THESE DAYS THE Wolves are very, very good to me. They give me two season tickets in the Bert Williams Suite and I'm very grateful for that. Sir Jack Hayward has been wonderful to us former players. He is so considerate and knows all our Christian names. He often comes to our dinners. He is a wonderful man.

I don't preach much to my family, but I do say to them, "If there's anything you want to do in life, then do it. You never know what's going to happen. There's no such thing as tomorrow." It's a pity you can't realise as a young person just how good life is and that it doesn't last forever. There's nothing worse in life than looking back in retrospect and wishing you'd done something. You've got to live every day and be grateful for it.

SAMMY SMYTH: BORN 25 FEBRUARY 1925, BELFAST; 116 GAMES, 43 GOALS

# Sammy Smyth

## Wolves 3 Leicester City 1
## FA Cup Final
## Saturday 30 April 1949

ON THE MORNING of the Cup Final at breakfast, Bill Shorthouse and I had a bit of a heated discussion, you know. I can't for the life of me remember what it was about, but he said something to me about, "You're a big-headed bastard" and I said, "Oh, very good"! What a way to start the day. Cup Final day! I remember there being a bit of a contretemps between the two of us. And it wasn't wise to cross Bill.

When we were practising we used to go to Goodyear and we'd be crossing the ball and heading the ball, different skills for different people. We'd then have an eight-a-side and, when it came to choosing sides by picking up shirts from one of two piles on the ground, if Bill picked a white shirt everyone else would fight for them as well. Because he would really bang into you, even if you were his team-mate. If you were on the other side for one of those games, God help you! He was a tough guy. A really tough guy.

I STARTED PLAYING in my native Belfast with the Boys Brigade and in the Church League; I suppose I was about 14 or 15. Then I played for Distillery seconds and graduated into their firsts when I was 16. But there was a problem. This was wartime and I was still only a youngster. There was an inter-city cup competition which continued throughout the war and Distillery were using mature Army players, who were actually pro footballers from the UK serving in Ireland and playing for them. But they couldn't take them on longer away trips, such as down into Southern Ireland. So that's when the manager used me. I got fed up with only playing on those away games. Finally, after I had played well and scored and we'd won, when the following week I was dropped, I demanded to know why and the manager told me that he preferred to select an English League player – George Drury, who played centre-forward for Arsenal. I was a bit disgruntled.

So then Linfield, one of the bigger clubs in Northern Ireland, and their manager asked me to play for them. I was still an amateur then so I could choose who I played for and Distillery didn't have any control over me. I say amateur. I would freely admit that I was a 'sham-ateur'. I was paid £6 a week in 1940 by Linfield. It went well for a few years, but then I had a tussle at Linfield with another good centre-forward; a fellow called Davy Walsh. He ended up going to England to turn pro like me. We vied for the centre-forward position. He was much quicker, I was slow. In fact watching Peter Crouch these days reminds me of me. I was about his pace, although I'm only 5ft 11in. So I think I looked faster!

I got to the stage when I was only playing for the reserve team and then one day an inside-forward didn't turn up and the reserve team manager asked me if I would play there and I said I would play anywhere. I went out and played a blinder and they wanted to put me in the first team. I was getting more space and time playing in midfield as you would call it today, as I wasn't suffering like centre-forwards do with tight marking, someone right up behind me. I played there for a couple of years. By this time I was 22. We were winning competitions and I was scoring and creating goals.

Then this guy came from Wolverhampton and asked me it I wanted to play for them. I thought he was pulling my leg, you know. The Wolves manager Ted Vizard came over and made an appointment with me to sign me up. We met in a pub and he said, "We can only give you £10 as a signing-on fee because you're an amateur." So I said, "I'm afraid you've wasted your journey." And he explained that there was a way around this. Wolves had an arrangement with a club called Dundella, who were in the minor league in Northern Ireland. He said, "You can sign for them as a professional and then we will sign you." I said I'd be looking for a £1,500 signing-on fee. It wasn't an extortionate amount, but he said no, you can have £1,100, but the income tax took a fair proportion so I got only £660. I presume Dundella received something for their troubles, but Linfield got nothing. I was persona non grata there, because I'd left that way.

MY FATHER HAD always told me, "Never join a club at the top, join a club who are getting better, so that you can be associated with the future success." I knew Wolves were on the way up. They had some great players and Ted Vizard was a gentleman. He impressed me. He was very badly treated at Wolves. At the end of that season, 47/48, he was sacked and Stan Cullis took over. We'd finished fifth in the league which isn't that bad. I didn't know what was going on at the time, but I now realise Cullis was always going to be made manager. He'd only retired as a player a couple of months before I joined the club after Wolves had just missed out on the title, by losing their last home game to Liverpool, who won the Championship instead.

I found out early on that Cullis wasn't exactly playing his role as Vizard's assistant how Ted would maybe have liked it. In September 1947 I was picked for Ireland because Peter Doherty was injured and I was brought in. I'd only been at

Wolves about a month. And we played against Scotland and we won 2-0 and I scored both goals. I went back to Molineux walking on air, you know. My agreement with Wolves was that when I was in the first team I got £11 a week and when I wasn't I got £9. So I get paid on the following Friday and I find I've only got £9. So I went to see Mr Vizard and said, "Mr Vizard, can I have a word with you. Why have I only got £9?" And he said, "By the terms of your contract you get £11 when playing in first team." I said "But if I hadn't been playing for Ireland I would have been in the first team." He said, "That is supposition, Sam. We don't know. So by your agreement we can legally only pay you £9. The FA wouldn't be happy and you can understand their point of view." Anyway Cullis heard about this, which I had actually accepted as Vizard was right and I'd been paid £10 to play for Ireland anyway. But Cullis tried to stir me up to complain to the board about how Vizard had treated me. I refused but Cullis went to the directors with any complaints there were. He was constantly talking to them and it was obvious what was going to happen. It had become a situation that you'd got this king in waiting. So Vizard was sacked.

At the time the club had the tag of being a "nearly team". They'd lost the Cup Final against Portsmouth in 1939 and in 1947 they'd lost the league on the last day. But I never thought that. I'm stupid enough to think that you've got to try hard and take your chances and you can control your own destiny, so I didn't believe all that guff. I was actually very immature. I was 22 and a virgin, I knew nothing about girls at all. My week in Ireland had consisted of Bible class, Christian Endeavours, Boys' Brigade and sports clubs, football and cricket. Girls didn't come into the equation until I went to Wolves. I shared my digs with Ted Elliott, the reserve team keeper. He was good with the girls, having served in the Navy, and he taught me a lot!

As soon as he took over as manager, Cullis put a notice above the dressing-room door which said, "There is no substitute for hard work." And do you know what I told him? I told him my father used to say to me "Hard workers should go down the mine!" Cullis was furious about that. But that was my father's attitude. He was a bookie and wanted the easiest way to the loaf. I'll never forget Cullis' face when I said that!

TRAINING WAS VERY hard, because I wasn't used to it – full time training. It was a shock. They tried to shorten my stride to make me move a bit quicker and we did it by trying not to walk on the cracks on the pavement! We weren't all like the superstars of today with four-wheel drives and limos, of our squad only Terry Springthorpe had a car, so I walked to and from my digs to the ground for training every day, learning to quicken my steps. And I went back for extra training in the afternoons. There used to be what we called the "dungeon" underneath the stands. It was a big dark room which we'd use to kick balls around and practise trapping and heading. Joe Gardiner would spend a lot of time in there with me. I would stand 20 yards from him with my back to him and he threw the ball off the walls and angles and I had ten yards to turn and trap it and shoot. It did work. It did improve me. But it used to wreck me. I used to fall asleep taking girls to the pictures – and that didn't help I can tell you!

I got into the team for the opening game of the 1947/48 season. I made my debut in place of Scotsman Willie Forbes and I started out as an inside-left at Maine Road. I scored my first goals in an 8-1 hammering of Grimsby in the first home game. I kept my place for a dozen games and then Vizard dropped me. But once Cullis came in as manager I was back, this time as inside-right. Jimmy Dunn, who I thought was our best player, was the other inside-forward. Wolves always started each match with a bang. It was our trademark. After 20 minutes if we hadn't scored, Jimmy would say to me, "We're bucked today again" and I would say, "Come on, let's keep going". Pye and Hancocks were outstanding too. What a forward line – apart from me! I had great anticipation. That was all I really had. Dunn would say to me, "You've got fingerprints on every goal post in the land" because I would move in to tidy up situations where a goalkeeper would make a save or the ball got blocked from a shot and came back out. That was how I got a lot of my goals. All the others could hit the ball very hard and it would come back out and I would score! But goalscoring is about being in the right place. Anticipation. It allowed to me top score the year we won the Cup with 22 goals.

We had one or two absolutely outstanding players in our team. Bert Williams in goal was an England international, Roy Pritchard the full-back was one of the best volleyers of the ball I had ever seen. It almost always went where he wanted it to go. Wright, Dunn, Hancocks. Mullen was so quick he was caught offside a lot because he was too quick for the linesman. If he'd had any confidence he would have scored a lot of goals, but he lacked the confidence to cut in and shoot. But he helped me score because of that. Because I knew he would get to the byline and cross. I was always going to the near post. That's how I scored a lot of my goals, you know. I scored all of my five international goals for Ireland that way. I watch football today and I see so many goals that could have been scored if the attacking forwards had timed their run to the near post. All you need to do is get there first and flick it or get a touch on it and you'd score.

It didn't always work, mind you. I remember once playing at Blackpool and the ball came across low and hard to me at the near post and I opened my legs and the ball went across the area, beating everyone and out for a throw in. Mr Cullis had something to say to me about that. But I just said, "I don't know who called behind me, but somebody did!"

The weakest links in the team were Terry Springthorpe, Billy Crook and myself. We *were* the weakest links, seriously. I'm not being self-effacing. It's just accurate. Eddie Russell was unfortunate. He was a super player, but Billy Crook was Cullis' favourite. He was tenacious, but very ordinary and we all wondered why Russell didn't get in the team. The year after we won the cup we went 13 games unbeaten. Bill Crook was injured and Eddie Russell came into the side. But Crook came straight back in afterwards when he was fit. I just couldn't fathom that.

Talking of great players and as a Northern Irishman, George Best was the best player I've ever seen in my time. Pelé, Matthews, Finney. They were all great players, but Best was extraordinary as a footballer. But he was also a lunatic, at least bordering on lunacy. Alright people say he had a disease, and alcoholism is a disease. But Best would often let people down because of the way he was. I had a friend who had about 200 boys, football-mad, between the ages of 11 and 14. And Best had agreed to come and talk to them. But he didn't arrive. So they rang up and he wasn't even in the country. He'd missed the plane from Manchester. He never apologised. He let so many people down. But the thing that annoyed me most about George Best was that he deprived me of watching him for another ten years. He was so far ahead of the rest of them. Gazza is another one. Wayne Rooney could go the same way if he doesn't steady himself down, going to brothels and the such-like. It seems like money corrupts everything. It did for Best and arguably Gazza. And that's the modern hierarchies. If you go for a job and they say, "We'll pay you 100,000 a week," you're not going to say, "No, only pay me 50." Are you?

CULLIS PUT ME back in the team from the start of the 1948/49 season. We finished sixth in the league that season, but we could score goals on our day. We won 5-0 at Bolton, I remember, and murdered Huddersfield 7-1. So it was no surprise when we hammered Division Two Chesterfield 6-0 in the third round of the FA Cup in January. I got a couple of goals that day, as did Jesse Pye. The FA Cup was always something special. You knew from as soon as you woke up in the morning that you *have* to win. We coasted through the fourth round too, beating Sheffield United 3-0. Johnny Hancocks scored two penalties that game; one with his right and one with his left, so he did. My God he could hit the ball and it never left the ground as it zipped into the net.

After beating Liverpool 3-1 we drew local rivals West Brom. That was a very hard game. They may have only been in the Second Division, but they won promotion that year. But we beat them 1-0 and Jimmy Dunn scored it. As a local derby it was huge. Jimmy didn't score many goals. I was playing against two Irish compatriots in the West Brom side Davy Walsh (who I'd vied for the centre-forward spot with at Linfield) and Jack Vernon.

As a run like that goes on you develop superstitions. I wore an old green shirt to the game, it was frayed around the edges, but I wore right up to the Cup Final. It wasn't an Irish thing really, just a colour that suited me. I hadn't heard about the story of Johnny Hancocks having to tie up Billy Wright's boot laces during that Cup run either. That I didn't see, but it may have happened.

SO THAT PUT us into the semi-finals. There were also Portsmouth and Leicester in the draw. We weren't bothered who we drew. You could have said we'd been unlucky if we got Portsmouth because they were the best team in the country. They won the league twice in a row in 48/49 and 49/50. But we drew Manchester United. That was tough enough. They were Cup holders having beaten Blackpool in the 1948 final.

At Wolves you were a chattel. They got the best people to make sure you were fit and in top playing condition because "we own you and you are going to do a good job for us". We had to do what we were told. The manager was fairly aloof. We used to come down to breakfast at hotels when we were on trips and Cullis would be already in the restaurant sitting reading a newspaper. As you walked into the restaurant from behind this newspaper you'd hear, "Morning, Sam," and the paper wouldn't move! And we'd say, "Morning, Stan." But the paper never twitched.

Cullis even used to charge you a penny for reading his newspaper on the bus. He really did. His theory was that if we wanted to read it we should buy the paper ourselves. He actually had a bit of an inferiority complex because he hadn't won anything as a player. And he wasn't too keen on us doing anything other than thinking about football. He wanted us to concentrate on the task in hand and not get distracted.

When we were playing away from home we would go to the pictures on a Friday night and no matter what the film was or who was in it, Stan had to have a different opinion. If the general consensus was that the film was a good one and that such and such an actor was good, then Stan would have to say that he didn't like it or them. He really did have to have the last word. But when it came to football, he so often was right.

Cullis gave us tactical talks, which we hadn't had very many of before with Vizard. He was also a more determined bloke. Vizard was too gentlemanly really. Cullis was a different cup of tea. He just wanted to see us working, not enjoying yourselves, not laughing, but that's not to say he wasn't a great manager. He knew about working out opposition teams. He was right about how to play United in those two semi-finals that year. They were a great side and we beat them using his tactics.

THE UNITED GAMES were epics, partly because of the injuries to our full-backs. I scored the first goal in the first game. I was about 18 yards out and I got the ball and set it up and had a go. It could have gone anywhere. When they go in from there they look like great goals, but often they'd fly wide or over by miles. Luckily that day it went in! I didn't celebrate like they celebrate goals today. What amazes me now is that they don't hurt one another all the time. All they have to do is land badly and they'd dislocate something. If I was the manager they wouldn't be doing all those things.

United equalised midway through the first half thanks to Charlie Mitten. It was backs to the wall for most of the rest of the game as we effectively only had nine players, but we survived. Laurie Kelly, who'd gone off injured in that first game, didn't recover and Cullis brought Terry Springthorpe in for the replay. Terry was a very tough guy. He knocked hell out of United's right winger, Delaney. I know Cullis and Busby had words about it by the benches during the game (it *was* actually a bench in those days). Stan was giving it all "get stuck in there" with Springthorpe and Busby didn't take kindly to that. Cullis was always getting up off his seat and shouting, a bit like Sir Alex Ferguson, you know. I remember one time later on I was sitting beside him, when Peter Broadbent had displaced me from the side. And I'd say to him, "Steady yourself, Stan. You're the manager of this side." And he'd say, "Don't speak to me like that". Pye missed this sitter. And Stan went mad shouting, "That's the Pye we know!" He would never swear though. He always said "flip". Flipping this and flipping that.

Cullis would encourage me to poach goals by popping up in the area. He'd say that keepers and defenders would take their eye off the ball and that's how I scored the winner in that semi-final replay. I had missed a sitter just before half-time. I'd had a good chance with a header and I had fluffed it. Cullis moaned at me for flicking at the ball. "Head it properly," he said "Get some meat on it." I said, "Don't worry, Stan. I'll not miss them all." Then Pye got the ball late on in the game on the right wing. He cut in and had a shot at goal. It hit the United goalkeeper, Bob Crompton, and fair bounced off my head and into the net.

THE FA CUP Final is the biggest game you will ever play and you're keyed up for it and very aware of it. I can't remember much about the two weeks leading up to the game. You just make sure you don't get injured when you know a final's coming up. Our league form wasn't great (Wolves lost 5-0 at Portsmouth in the run up to Wembley). Both our full-backs were injured and Pye had been injured in that replay. There was a lot of uncertainty about who would actually play in the Final.

One of the most important things about getting to Wembley for all the players in those days was to be able to make a bit of extra cash out of our success. We asked a photographer to take some pictures of us and we had some cards made up for sixpence each. Then we got programme sellers to buy them off us for ninepence and they sold them to fans for a shilling. We did well out of that, although it was a nightmare to collect all the money in. One programme seller even tried to sell one photo of myself to me! I also decided we would have a dance to celebrate the Final and that we would place the markings of a football field on the floor of the Civic Hall. We used the same lime that they used for the markings at Molineux and we put some goalposts up at either end. When we printed the tickets we said on them that we had a licence, but we didn't. We hadn't even applied for one at that stage and one of the Wolves directors, a Mr Oakley I think, got wind of this and, because he was on the council, I had to ask him to sort it out for us. He kept me on the edge of my seat making me think it was touch and go whether he would say "no", but he eventually agreed. All 16 players in the squad got £47 each for that event. And I'd organised it all more or less myself. We also managed to give £54 to a blind charity near Molineux.

THE MAIN TALKING points were really who was going to play. In Jesse Pye's absence the young Dennis Wilshaw had come into the side and scored ten goals in 11 games. He'd really staked his claim, but Stan Cullis went with experience and chose Pye in the end. Dennis never played in an FA Cup Final, although he did have a Wembley magic moment when he scored five goals in an international there – and against Scotland too.

Then there was the full-back situation. Both Billy Crook and Laurie Kelly were fit again now and so Cullis had to make a choice. When we got on to the coach to travel down to London on the Friday we didn't know who would be playing. And it wasn't until we got to Oxford that we discovered that Cullis has given Billy Wright, the captain, the job of telling Kelly that he wasn't going to be playing as Springthorpe was in. Remember there were no substitutes then so you were either in or out, no halfway house on the bench. Laurie didn't take it well and got off the bus when it pulled up at a red light in Oxford. I said to him, "Don't be ridiculous, Lol. You don't know where you are." But got off he did, although he did come to the game with his wife.

I DIDN'T FORGET the argument with Bill Shorthouse in the morning, but tension was high, you know. We were such big favourites. Leicester were facing relegation from the Second Division (they only secured their status with three points from three games after the FA Cup Final). It was the same situation that Wolves had faced in the '39 upset when Portsmouth beat Wolves 4-1. Cullis, of course, having played in that Final, kept reminding us about it. I think it had hurt him a lot and he wasn't going to let us forget that we had a task to complete. Leicester's best player, Don Revie, the centre-forward, was not fit. He'd burst a blood vessel in his nose three days before the Final. We didn't think about it particularly, but it obviously wasn't good news for them. We always thought we would win the game. We had a tactical talk from Stan, what he thought were their strengths and weaknesses. He liked a spot of theorising and he was very often accurate.

Before the game, while we waited for what seemed like an eternity, Kenneth Wolstenholme, the great commentator, asked me if my name was pronounced Smith or Smyth and I replied, "I don't care as long as that's all they call me!" In actual fact my name is pronounced plain Smith. But once people started putting the Y into it when I arrived at Wolves, it was impossible to explain it to everyone, so I'd just had to go along with being called Smyth.

The hymn, *Abide With Me*, it got to me you know. I'm very emotional about music and that hymn got to me. And in those days they had a singer who led the community singing before we went out, so you could hear it in the dressing room clearly. We met Princess Elizabeth, who of course is now Queen, in the line-up and shook hands with her. She was wearing a blue dress and apparently all the talk was of how she was rooting for Leicester, because that was their colour. I didn't really notice that, but put it this way I didn't tackle her!

It was my first visit to Wembley. I'd never even been there to watch a match. I was so focussed that I didn't hear the crowd, seriously.

WE PLAYED REALLY well in the first half. Typical Wolves. A bludgeoning start. Not many mistakes; efficient and fast. Jesse scored our first goal with a stooping header from Hancocks' cross. He actually very rarely headed the ball, but on that occasion he headed it into the net to give us the lead. The second goal was interesting because both Jesse and I struck at the ball at the same time and it ended up going into the net. He ran off celebrating, but I thought I'd hit it. After the game he was adamant that he had scored it, so I just said, "It doesn't matter who scored it because we won."

At half-time we were 2-0 up and Stan was warning us not to be complacent; that we needed another goal to be sure. Of course we went straight out and they scored then. Bert Williams saved Chisholm's shot, but Griffiths put the rebound in off the post. That was just like the type of goal that I usually scored! We were looking quite wobbly for a moment there.

We were under the cosh a bit and Billy Wright proved what a tremendous player he was by repelling everything Leicester could throw at us. His blond head seemed to pop up everywhere.

The next thing I saw was the ball hitting the back of our net again. And I thought "Oh God!", but then I realised that the referee had given offside. I thought they'd equalised. I didn't realise until the referee gave it. It was Chisholm again. He was standing about a body's width ahead of the last defender. They tried to argue that it had come off a Wolves player last, but I don't think so. In the heat of the moment you don't really know. I only know he really *was* offside because I saw a photo later. It was close but he was offside.

Then I was lucky enough to score the goal that I did. I collected the ball about the centre circle on our left flank and started running towards goal. Normally when I got the ball in those areas I wanted to part with it, because I hadn't the speed to make a dent in opposing defences. Roger Byrne, the Manchester United full-back, who sadly died in the Munich crash, used to tackle me twice. If I got past him the first time he was quick enough to catch me up and tackle me again. I used to say to him, "Roger. For God's sake. Once you're beaten can you stay beaten!"

So as I ran I was intending to kick it left to Dunn or whoever was shouting on the wing and then I feinted to pass it the other way, right, and all the time I was running towards the goal. At my pace, which was not particularly quick, I think the Leicester players thought I'd have to pass. The only player I can really remember beating was the centre-half, Plummer. And he was the last in line. I teed it up by jinking to my left and hit it with the foot I stand on. I'm serious! I never shot with my left foot and I hit it really well and it went right across the goalkeeper and into the corner of the net. He dived, but he had no chance.

The lads had done a tremendous job as I moved forwards with the ball, drawing the Leicester players away with their runs. Afterwards Jimmy Dunn said, "Sammy, they kept running away from you." And I said, "I appreciate that." That was because the goal was made by others making runs and drawing Leicester players off, allowing me to keep going.

Cullis, every time I met him after that, used to say, "I'll never forget that goal" and I say, "No, neither will I", but in a sense it was a fluke. I hadn't really scored a goal like that from 25 yards before. Mine were all close range goals, well within the 18-yard box. That's the only goal I can ever remember scoring like that. I don't even know why I went to beat the centre-half to his right and hit it with my left. It all happened so fast, but I suppose it's a matter of his balance, my balance, our relative speeds, I don't know really. Whatever way he was standing. But it worked out nicely didn't it? That's fortune you know, to turn the right way. If I'd gone on my normal foot I'd have turned straight into him wouldn't I? It's one of those things. And it was called the 'finest goal ever seen at Wembley'. That may or may not be true, but when the ball hit the back of the net it was unbelievable. A great cheer and I can't remember what I did.

If that had happened in a reserve match then no one would have bothered with it or even known about it, but it happened at Wembley in the biggest showpiece of all. My father and mother were at the game and they were all cheering and my mother turned to my father and said, "What's he done now?!" Unbelievable!

That killed Leicester off then. They hadn't got anything left to give. They'd had two hammer blows in about three minutes. One goal disallowed and then to concede to go two behind. It was game over.

We went up to get our medals. And now I haven't got mine. It was stolen by someone who broke into my house and I've never had it back. My son rang the FA to get a replacement, but they said, "No". I suppose that's one of those things.

After a celebration dinner that night at the Café Royale, coming back to Wolverhampton the next day was colossal. I said at the time, "It must be really terrible to lose." Imagine missing a gilt-edged chance and losing the Cup Final. That could be why Cullis was so desperate to win. He'd missed out on all the glory as a player himself.

My glory was obvious from the great reception I got. But still I think 'finest goal ever seen at Wembley'? It really was a bit of a fluke. The luck of the Irish!

ROY SWINBOURNE: BORN 25 AUGUST 1929, DENABY MAIN; 230 GAMES, 114 GOALS

# Roy Swinbourne

## Wolves 4 West Bromwich Albion 4

## FA Charity Shield

## Saturday 29 September 1954

I WAS BORN in a Yorkshire mining village called Denaby and signed amateur forms for Huddersfield Town as a 15 year-old. I used to travel by bus on a Saturday morning to Heckmondwyke, near Dewsbury, to play for their youth side. I also played in the Sheffield and Hallamshire representative team and we always had scouts knocking on the door. It was playing for them that I changed from a winger to a more central position. I was selected in the Possibles versus the Probables team. The lad who played outside-right for the other team had a great game and was the best player on the park. At half-time, while I was thinking, "Oh, I'm not going to get picked in the team ahead of him," our coach asked me to go to play inside-right alongside this other lad and we gelled really well and so I was no longer an outside-right any more.

Because I was an amateur it meant I could change club in the summer, although we were tied during the winter from August through to May. Wolves had this junior team called Wath Wanderers in Yorkshire, which they used as a nursery club to bring on talent in the area. It was run by an old Wolves pro called Mark Crook and Wolves used to sponsor the balls and shirts. I signed for them and Mark would occasionally take us down to Wolverhampton in his car to play in the A team or B team so Ted Vizard, who was then manager, could take a look at us. At 16 Wolves said, "We want you to come down and live in Wolverhampton." I asked my Dad what he thought and he said, "Well, if you can make it at Wolves you can make it anywhere." In those days Wolves and Manchester United were the two clubs renowned for encouraging Juniors. So I agreed to join them as an amateur for one year to see how it went. I also had offers from Sunderland and various other clubs. I decided I'd rather do that than stay with Huddersfield. My Dad, Tom, was from Birmingham and had been on Aston Villa's books although he hadn't made it as a pro. He was player-manager of Denaby United at the time. So he wasn't too worried about me coming to the Midlands.

So I caught a train to Wolverhampton. I got out of the station and asked the taxi driver, "Can you take me to Wolves, please?" And he said, "Oh, no. Not another one!" I think he was fed up with ferrying the hundreds of youngsters who came for trials the short distance from the station to the ground. It didn't make him a lot of money!

When I arrived, Jack Howley welcomed me and told me, "You'll be staying with Mrs Nooth at 86 Evans Street." There were two senior pros lodging there, Roy Pritchard, the left-back, and Angus McLean, the centre-half. They were avoiding doing military National Service by working as Bevin Boys at Hilton Main colliery. It was perfectly legal, but meant they weren't often around. That night I had some tea. And when Angus and Roy had finished training, which they had to do after work, they came in and said "Alright youngster. How are you doing?" Angus told me he was going out with Doreen, his girlfriend that night, but Roy asked me "What are you doing tonight?" I'd obviously only just arrived, so I didn't know anywhere to go, so he said "You'd better come with me then." We went out and had something to eat and then he said, "Right, we'll have a treat now." I got all excited. "We'll go to the dogs at Monmoor Green." So on my first night as a Wolves player I went to watch this dog race meeting! But he always looked after me did Roy.

I started playing in the Worcester Combination and the Birmingham League. They would have been about the third or fourth teams. I think the club had nine at the time. A huge number of players. I remember on a Saturday morning when we all had to meet to get on coaches to go to our respective games, there were hundreds of men and boys trying to find the right bus to get on. It was mayhem! But it was alive and buzzing really. We used to get on so well with the tea ladies and it felt like a family. The reserves used to win the Central League every year. They certainly won it three years in a row when I played in it a couple of years later. The club was so strong.

Then the first team won the Cup in 1949 and that spurred everyone on. Wolves was a great club and we all wanted to be involved in winning things, but I missed out on much of the next two years because of National Service. I did my square bashing up at Manchester and then I took what was called an "Adaption Test", which checked your aptitude for various jobs. I did quite well in it and the Sergeant asked me what I wanted to do. I requested to be a PTI (physical training instructor). But that meant signing on for three years, and I wanted to get back to playing as quickly as possible, so I then asked to be posted as an aircraft fitter or engine fitter because the training for both of these was done at Cosford. The sergeant said, "Actually you've got to pick three, but don't worry. You'll be alright." He understood that if I was posted to Cosford I could still play for Wolves much of the time. So I said, "Put me down for electrician." And of course what comes through but electrician. So I ended up being posted miles away in Melksham, Wiltshire and there was no way back to Molineux. I did try it as the Sergeant used to arrange that I could leave base on a Friday night. But I had to thumb a lift. There was no M5, no buses, so I used to go outside the camp, thumb a lift to Bristol and then try to pick up someone coming up the A38. I used to get into Wolverhampton in the early hours ready to play the next day. But that's how it was.

I also played cricket for the camp. After I'd completed my training as an electrician, my final posting came through and it was just down the road from Melksham. The guy who was the captain of the cricket team was also the camp medical officer. He asked me to come and see him and looked me up and down and said, "That knee, Roy. It looks bad." So he declared me unfit for posting! So I played cricket for his team all summer and waited for a posting to come through closer to Wolverhampton. Eventually Tern Hill came through, near Market Drayton. And so I went there, which was much easier to get back to play.

By the time I came out of the Forces I was coming up to 20. I'd played in the RAF with West Brom's legendary England forward Ronnie Allen. He was the best volleyer of the ball I have ever seen. He could volley a ball at knee height and keep it low so it didn't go over the top. It used to whistle into the net. With Ronnie as right winger I played centre-forward and scored a lot of goals thanks to his crosses. We had a good RAF team, but I was happy to get out and get back to playing for Wolves properly.

BY NOW I was playing in the reserves. The season after Wolves had won the Cup they went on a terrible run and Cullis decided to change his team. He'd become manager after Vizard left, so I got the nod when he dropped Sammy Smyth. And I came in as an inside-right. I was the first of the youngsters to be drafted into the team. I stayed in the team for a few games and then Jesse Pye moved to Luton in 1952 and I moved from inside-right to centre-forward.

I was lucky to be playing in a team which boasted Hancocks, Mullen, Wilshaw and Broadbent as I got plenty of chances. It was a great team, you know. If you can't play in a team like that, you can't play. It went well and I adapted to centre-forward. Johnny Hancocks used to love to come in the middle looking for goals, while Jimmy Mullen always used to get to the dead-ball line. And if I couldn't get to his cross I would hear Johnny behind me saying, "Right, Swindy." And I would duck under it and he would hit the ball. Bang. And it would fly in. I suppose I was a bit different to Jesse Pye as I was taller. He was very quick and a good poacher. I was more of a straight-forward frontman.

Peter Broadbent was a great playmaker as well. I fitted into that by moving out on to the right wing. Johnny would come inside and that made us very fluid and confused defenders. Jimmy Mullen, however, always stuck to the line. Peter would float around in the middle and play us in. Then Dennis Wilshaw would fill the gaps in the middle if I moved out on to the wing. He scored plenty of goals too. In later years I would show Dennis photographs of games and it was always me fighting for the ball and him unmarked waiting for it to break free. So I would say to him, "Look, Dennis. There you are again, waiting for the snips!" He was a lovely man and we had a laugh. In fact the whole team had a strong bond.

It meant we were a formidable side to play against. I remember beating Cardiff away 9-1 in 1955. I felt sorry for them because everything we did that day turned to gold. I scored one cheeky backheel of the kind that only goes in once in a blue moon. That was a phenomenal result, but by that time we were well used to success.

IN 1953 OUR team had built up to being one of the most feared in the country. It was based on the confidence we had, because we always went on to the pitch in a positive mood, thinking we were going to win. We felt there was no one who could beat us. It wasn't arrogant, it was just how it was. And we scored a few goals too. It was a brilliant atmosphere. That season we beat Chelsea 8-1 and Sheffield United 6-1. Goals flew in all over the place. And the rest of the team wasn't bad. The half-back line was Slater, Wright and Flowers and Bill Shorthouse was solid at full-back with Eddie Stuart adding grit too. Then there was Bert Williams in goal, who was just the best as far as I was concerned.

It was touch and go between us and West Brom for the title, which made it even more special as the local rivalry stirred things up even more. We went to the Hawthorns in April for a big game, which effectively would decide the destiny of the title. I got the goal as we won 1-0. It was a cross from the right and I went in and flicked it with my head and scored. That really clinched it for us. We still needed some more points, but it was nigh on impossible for them to catch us after that. It was like four points to us. Albion were a very good side and could have done the double that year. They had Ronnie Allen of course, Jimmy Dugdale at centre-half, Ray Barlow in midfield, Davy Walsh, the Irish centre-forward. In the end we won the league and they won the FA Cup, which meant we met again just into the next season for the Charity Shield.

The Wolves fans came up with a song to sing about our victories over the Albion, which came to be heard on the terraces, particularly from the South Bank over the next few years. Chanting was relatively new then and so this one sticks in my mind. It went:

*Who's the team, the Wonder team*
*The team in gold and black*
*They knocked four points off the Albion*
*And beat Honved and Spartak*

Stan Cullis would not stand for any cowardice as a manager. You had to be committed. You went in to win the ball. None of this shirking or pulling out. He was dedicated – all for the Wolves, as it were. He used to live the game and kick every ball with you from the bench. Technically he was very good too and he knew the game inside out. He was always trying to get the best out of you, that little bit more that you could give which could make the difference. He had a great foil in Joe Gardiner. Joe would come in and calm people down after Stan had maybe had a go a little bit too much. But I liked Stan because his heart was in the right place. He always looked after his players, made sure your digs or club house were OK. And he would come training with us and you could see he'd been a good payer. He was good on the ball.

We actually clinched the 1953/54 championship by beating Spurs, one of our other rivals, 2-0. We used to love to play them as, with their 'push and run' style, we always though they were fragile and we could overpower them. They really didn't like the fact we closed them down. They wanted time on the ball and we wouldn't give it to them. Cullis loved that day, because he had been so close to wining the Championship as a player. He was delighted. And it was a great day for the town. In those days the football club *was* the town. After training we would go to Lyon's Corner House for coffee and chat for people. These days the players get in their cars and planes and helicopters and they're gone. There's no sense of belonging.

In fact Stan was quite strict on that kind of stuff. He went so far as to produce this little book of rules. It had a red cover, so it was Stan's Red Book. A bit like Chairman Mau's! We weren't actually allowed to have cars, because he thought driving to the ground on a matchday would restrict your movement and also was too risky in case of crashes or breakdowns. So he insisted we either catch a bus or walk to the ground. I wish I'd kept a copy of the book as there were a lot of dos and don'ts. Most of them were very sensible, such as no dancing after Wednesday night. That was fair enough both from an injury point of view and also as he didn't want us socialising on the evenings before the game. He had his spies in the town who would tell him if players were out drinking on a Thursday or Friday night. If anyone fell foul of the rules for say drinking he would ask Joe to get them to come to see him. He would have you in and say, "Look, I don't mind you having a drink, but not before a game."

The town was delighted when we finally won the league. That was what they had craved for so long. They'd lost the Cup in '39 and then the League in '47, so this triumph was special. Wolves had always been thought of as one of the best sides in the country, but they'd not proved it had they? Apart from the '49 Cup Final they hadn't won anything for years. So that title was particularly special.

IN THOSE DAYS the Charity Shield was played a few weeks into the season, rather than as a curtain raiser. Because we were one of the few clubs who had floodlights, we hosted the match at Molineux. Both teams were hit by injuries and loss of players to international duty. We missed Billy Wright and Bill Slater, while the Baggies lost Ray Barlow who were all in Ireland to play in the international there, while Eddie Stuart, Roy Pritchard and Jimmy Mullen were all injured, so Dennis Wilshaw ended up playing outside-left and Peter Russell made his debut at centre-half.

It was a cracking game. Ronnie Allen got three and I got two. It felt more like an exhibition game. It must have been fantastic to watch. Both my goals came from shots near the edge of the area, while Norman Deeley scored with a flick header, which wasn't bad for a lad of his height!

Strangely that night there were actually substitutes allowed for injuries. I think it was some kind of experiment on the FA's behalf. They were only allowed to come on for injured players as I remember. I don't think we had anyone left to bring on anyway actually, but Albion used two subs, who became the first ever at Molineux. I remember Bill Shorthouse being severely lectured by the referee for one strong tackle which led to Lee, their winger, going off. That was about a strong as referees got in those days.

The main controversy of this wonderful night's football came right at the death with the scored locked at 4-4. Albion won an indirect free kick from which Ronnie Allen blasted a shot through our wall and past Bert. It would have been his fourth goal and surely a winning one, but the referee decided that Jimmy Dudley, who had taken the free kick – it was indirect remember - had not made the ball move. He had just touched it with his boot and the referee deemed it not to have been in play and so they could not score from it. It was a bizarre thing really, but there wasn't anything we could do about it so we thanked our lucky stars and got on with it.

There was no animosity at all amongst the players. In fact in general we were very happy when the Albion won things, as long as it wasn't against us. We always wanted to win the games between us, but outside that we were very supportive of each other really.

They had wingers called Lee and Griffin who were rivalling Hancocks and Mullen, while I played directly against Joe Kennedy and he was the nicest centre-half I've ever come across. Plenty of others would whack your ankles on purpose or bad mouth you, but Joe ("Spring-heeled Joe", we used to call him) was a gentleman. He was in it for the Sport. He wanted to win, don't get me wrong, but he wasn't rough and he liked to play football. For a centre-half I would actually call him gentle.

The biggest thing under floodlights was the ball. We weren't allowed to play with a different ball for league matches under Football League rules, but as this wasn't a league game we played with a forerunner of the plastic ball they use today. It was the same against Honved. You could do things with that ball, you could bend it. You couldn't do that with the Football League ball. I feel sorry for goalkeepers today as the ball is so light and moves around so much. The leather ball we used for league games was so heavy and hard. It was difficult to strike it sweetly, but if Johnny Hancocks did catch it right you'd better get out of the way!

I remember him in training. He was only small, but he had huge calf muscles. He would put balls on the 18 yard line and hit the left post, then the right post, then the crossbar. He was very accurate. He could be devastating too. I remember playing Arsenal at Molineux and Johnny took their left-back to pieces. He turned him inside out. The guy just couldn't do anything. Towards the end of the game Johnny went past him yet again and the poor fellow just looked at the crowd and stretched out his arms as if to say, "What can I do"! Those are lovely memories.

I also remember our first European adventure. We toured Russia, I think we were the first English club to do so. We had to fly out to Helsinki, because in those Cold War days of the early 1950s you couldn't fly directly into Russia. We had to stay in Finland and then wait for an escort and a Russian plane to take us in. I don't think we had a military escort or anything like that, but you never really knew who was watching.

We lost at Spartak 3-0 and Dynamo 3-2. It was a bit unfair as we went out there in August which was actually halfway through their season, because they had to play in the summer to avoid the harsh winters. We had hardly trained after out summer break, so we weren't ready really. But when they'd played at our place in the November of the previous season it had been a different story. They'd just finished their season, but we were just really getting into our game and we beat Spartak 4-0.

STAN CULLIS HAD these unusual ways of motivating you. I remember at the start of the 1955/56 season I was having a shower after training and Stan came in and said, "How old are you now, Roy?" And I said, "I've only just turned 26 Mr Cullis." He said, "Well, I'll have to be thinking about getting a replacement"! I didn't know what to say. That was Stan and his inverse psychology.

You could say it worked, as everything was shaping up so well at the beginning of that season. I'd scored 17 goals in the 12 games, including three hat-tricks, and the team was flying. But Stan's little gee up for me turned out to be a little closer to the truth than I wanted. We played at Preston in early December and I took this ball down on my chest and shielded it from Tommy Docherty, who was coming in to tackle me, by turning away from him. But I was still in the process of bringing the ball down and the studs of my right boot caught in the turf as I landed, while the rest of my body twisted. I felt the knee wrench.

I had three operations to try and sort out the damage, but things weren't the same in those days as they are today and you couldn't recover so well from ligament injuries. So I had to retire a year later or so aged 26, when I'd had two or three goes at coming back. It was one of those things really. No one's fault. Docherty had actually been nowhere near me when it happened.

I was once told by a selector that I was going to be playing against Denmark for England in Copenhagen. I was told on a Sunday. For some reason, just after that, the FA decided that only two players from any one club would travel. And so Billy [Wright] and Bert [Williams] went and I was left behind. I never got picked again. Nat Lofthouse was the man the selectors preferred with Tommy Taylor getting a chance occasionally. I used to listen to the team being announced on the radio, listening for my name to be read out, but it was always that Lofthouse! The form I was in when my injury happened would have meant I would have been in with a chance of a recall I suppose, but it wasn't to be.

It's a shock when something like that happens and suddenly you have to make your own way. I got £500 compensation from the Players' Union and Wolves allowed me to buy my club house for the same price they'd paid for it several years earlier. I even had one room redecorated courtesy of the club! After I'd retired I joined Goodyear on the sales staff and then started my own tyre company, which went very well. I sold out when I retired a few years ago, so I suppose I had a sort of second life after playing for Wolves. But it was a huge help to get your foot in the door and be able to say, "Hello. My name's Roy Swinbourne of Wolverhampton Wanderers." It still sounds special to be able to say that today.

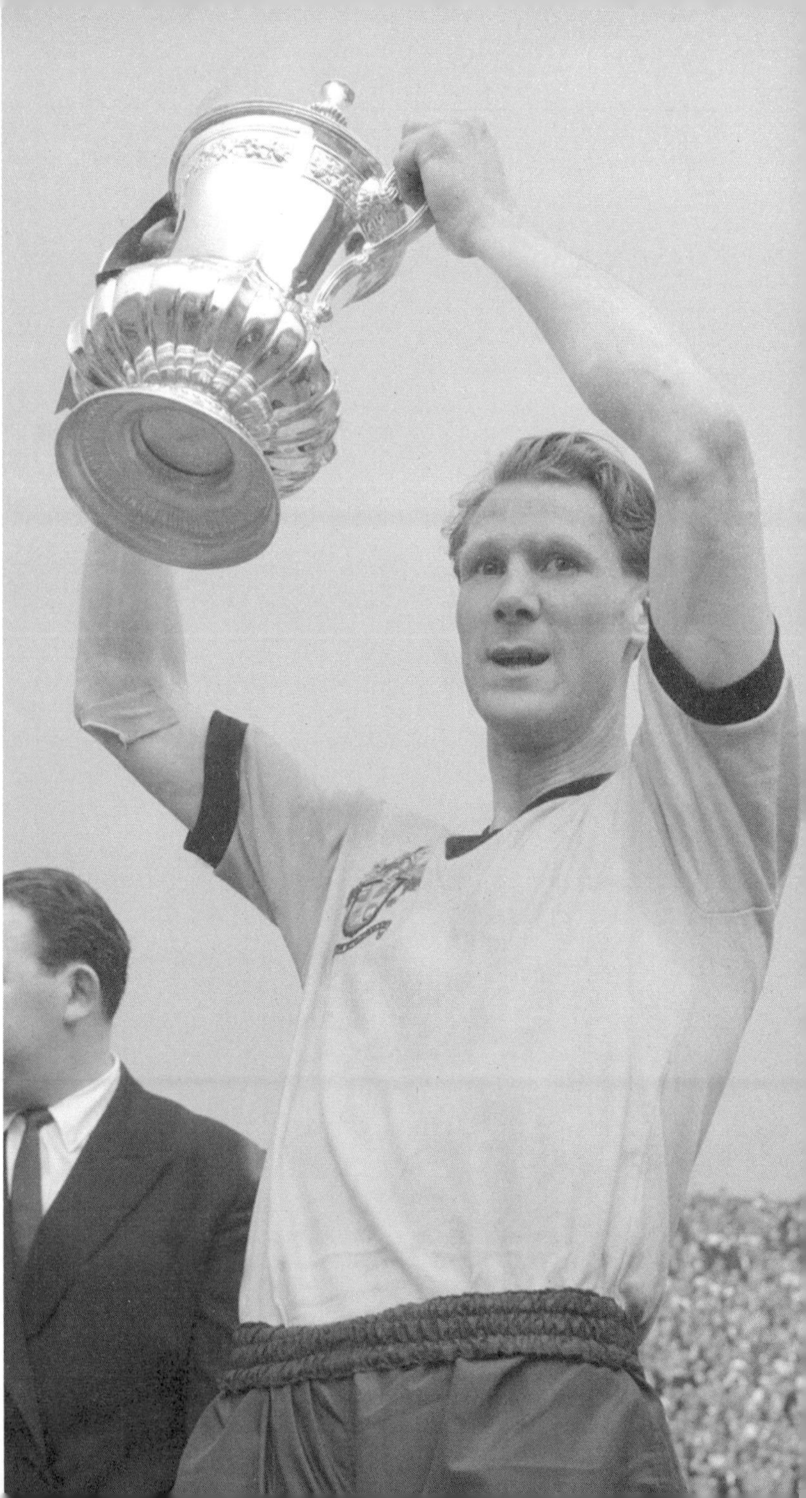

BILL SLATER: BORN 29 APRIL 1927, CLITHEROE; 339 GAMES, 25 GOALS

# Bill Slater

## Wolves 3 Honved 2

## European friendly

## Monday 13 December 1954

DURING MY FOOTBALL career I was not always a full-time professional and as a result my life was very different from that of most other Football League players. It didn't mean that I cared less for the game, in fact I was passionate about my football, but my other career in teaching was also important to me and I enjoyed my 'double life'. I doubt if two such careers would be possible today.

I began my football career on leaving school in 1943 aged 16 with Blackpool's Junior team. At that time, because of the war, with many senior players called up into the Armed Services, there were opportunities for young players to progress into the senior team more quickly than in peacetime.

My first game in the senior team was in unusual circumstances. I was also a keen cricketer and a member of the Blackpool Cricket Club. On this particular Saturday in the late summer, when the cricket and football seasons overlap, the cricket match in which I was playing was abandoned early due to rain and I received an urgent telephone message to report as quickly as possible by taxi to Bloomfield Road where Blackpool were taking on Preston North End with only ten available players. On reaching the ground I changed quickly from my cricket whites into football strip and emerged from the players' tunnel 15 minutes after kick-off to enormous cheers! Blackpool were already leading 2-0, despite only having ten men and went on to win 8-1.

The Blackpool team had several international players at that time, including Stanley Matthews at outside-right, Stanley Mortensen and captain Harry Johnston and I was instructed to play inside-right as partner to Stanley Matthews. But the coaching I had received at school did not fit well with his style of play and at half-time he explained to me in a kindly manner how I could avoid 'getting in his way'.

ON LEAVING SCHOOL I worked for a couple years in a bank prior to call up into the Army. I started as a post boy sorting mail and then progressed to the upkeep of customers' accounts. At that time this was by hand; computer records came much later. The only mechanical aid was an adding machine. It had an enormous lever which had to be pulled, with some difficulty by female members of staff, each time a figure was entered.

I spent three years in the Army, much of it in the Army Physical Training Corps at its headquarters in Germany preparing physical training instructors. The wars in Europe and the Far East were then over and there was plenty of opportunity for football and cricket. But I didn't enjoy Army life and was pleased to become a civilian again.

Rather than return to banking I decided instead to try for a career in teaching physical education and almost immediately began three years of studies in Leeds. I rejoined Blackpool as an amateur and played in the First Division of the Football League, but also played cricket too. Being in Leeds meant I could only turn out for either club when my studies allowed. Sometimes the football club arranged for me to travel to Blackpool by hired car; the cost must have been greater than the weekly wage of the professional players! On

Saturday mornings I often had to attend practical gymnastics classes and I became highly skilled at appearing as though I was working hard, when really I was saving all my energies for playing Manchester United or Liverpool later that day.

In 1951 I played for Blackpool in the FA Cup Final as a replacement for Allan Brown, the Scottish international, who unfortunately had broken a leg in the semi-final against Spurs. I think I may have been the last amateur to play in the Cup Final. I wouldn't have been playing had that not happened. We lost 2-0 to Newcastle, both goals scored by Jackie Milburn just after half-time. I was still at college and I had to be back in Leeds by midnight, so I caught the train from King's Cross as quickly as I could after the match, missing the club dinner. By chance the train was proceeding on from Leeds through to Newcastle and was packed with noisy, celebrating United supporters. Fortunately I found a corner seat in one of the compartments, kept my head down and wasn't recognised.

IN THE SUMMER of 1951 I met my wife Marion. She was attending a lawn tennis coaching course at Loughborough College, while I was taking an FA coaching course there. Those of us on the football course were invited to act as guinea pig pupils for the ladies on the tennis course to practise teaching on and I found myself being coached by Marion. I must have been a well-behaved and attentive pupil because a year later she married me! She lived in Ealing, London, teaching at a school there and, following completion of my teacher training in Leeds, I had been appointed to a post in the physical education department of Birmingham University, so in order to see Marion I travelled to London at weekends.

But I was keen also to continue playing football and decided to approach Brentford, whose Griffin Park ground was only a short bus ride from Ealing. Remember I was an amateur so at the end of each season my registration reverted to me and it was then my choice as to which club I signed up for the new season with. The attendant I met at the entrance to the club's offices was reluctant to allow me in until I explained that I had a few weeks earlier played in the Cup Final at Wembley. The club manager, Jack Gibbons, was more welcoming and, after a couple of games in the reserves, I was selected at wing-half for the first team, well placed at the time in the Second Division. Jackie had said that he wouldn't guarantee me a game in the first team, but I soon found myself playing regularly alongside the other half-back, Jimmy Hill and centre-half Ron Greenwood, later to manage the England team. Once I began playing in the first team the club kindly paid my Birmingham to London train fare.

Brentford was a happy, friendly club, but when in 1952 Marion and I married and settled in Birmingham I had no reason to visit London any more and Jack Gibbons gave me an introduction to Wolverhampton Wanderers. It was an eventful year. In addition to marriage and joining Wolves, I was selected for the Great Britain amateur football team, participating in the 1952 Olympic Games in Helsinki and had a first sight of the wonderful Hungarian players, who won that Olympic football tournament.

ON MY FIRST meeting with Stan Cullis, Wolves' manager, I made the mistake of indicating to him that I greatly enjoyed football and would be pleased to play in any of the club's teams. This brought a strong and lengthy rebuke that there was 'no place at the Wolves club for any player who does not have ambition to play in the first team'! He gave me an hour's lecture on this. Ambition and so forth. I always wondered what would have happened if I'd gone in and demanded to play in the first team. I asked him a few years later. Cullis said, "I think you'd have had a two hour lecture on being so forward!"

Stan was a dedicated, demanding manager, but at the same time he was sensitive to the interests and well-being of the players. When Marion had to spend several months in hospital, he was helpful to me in a number of ways. Joe Gardiner was the senior coach at the club, always approachable and encouraging, who made up an ideal pairing with Stan Cullis. He always gave me a good massage before home games so I would get in early on a Saturday. He was a lovely man, who, like Stan Cullis, never swore.

I was able to join the other Wolves players for the pre-season preparations, much of which took place during the university summer vacation, but mostly I had to train on my own at the university when teaching commitments allowed. I was fortunate because there was plenty of time for me within my schedule to find an hour to work on my fitness, so I could do marking, for example, maybe later in the evening. I developed a set of running routines on the campus playing field to maintain stamina and speed, using the clock on the university's central tower for timing. There were short, but steep, green steep slopes along one side of the field and I devised routines of repeat sprinting up them and walking back down. Nearby there was also a stretch of high wall with an uneven surface and I performed rebound drills against it for half an hour at a time. The ball rebounded at unexpected angles and heights to test my ball control. I tried to keep my training interesting and varied as I was on my own. Sometimes I would arrange to play a hard game of squash on one of the university courts after I'd finished my individual training in order to maintain my competitive edge. Not being able to train with playing colleagues throughout the season was not ideal, but the Wolves' style of play was direct and uncomplicated and I never felt out of touch with colleagues during matches.

I GAINED A place in the Wolves first team fairly soon after joining the club. My debut was at-right-half against Manchester United in place of Billy Wright, who was absent playing for England. Wolves won 6-2 before a large Molineux crowd and the Wolverhampton *Express and Star* jokingly suggested that Billy now retire!

He didn't, of course, but soon afterwards Billy switched to centre-half with Ron Flowers and myself filling the wing-half positions. Of the Wolves team in the early 1950s, goalkeeper Bert Williams, the three half-backs, Peter Broadbent and Dennis Wilshaw, and wingers Johnny Hancocks and Jimmy Mullen all at different times, represented England. If injury had not required him to retire early from football then surely centre-forward Roy Swinbourne would surely have done so too. Later in the 50s, wing-half Eddie Clamp and winger Norman Deeley also represented England. In the 1958 World Cup in Sweden, for most of the tournament the England team's half-back line was Clamp, Wright and myself – three Wolves players.

During the eight seasons 1952-1960, Wolves were Football League champions on three occasions and runners-up or third placed in all other seasons with the exception of 1956/57 when we finished fifth. In several of those seasons the team scored more than 100 league goals in the 42-match programme, an average of 2½ per match. During 1953/54, when Wolves became League Champions for the first time, I signed for the club as a part-time professional. A special clause in my Wolves contract stated that if a clash occurred between my university teaching commitments and selection for Wolves, the university teaching would have priority. But I missed only a few matches. The introduction of floodlights, which meant that evening kick-offs could start as late as 8pm, was of great help.

One Wolves match I did miss was the last midweek match of the 1955/56 season against Sheffield United. At that time

Bramall Lane doubled as a county cricket ground and did not have floodlights, so kick-off for the match was due to be in the early evening, meaning it was not possible for me to reach Sheffield by car or train after finishing afternoon lectures. So Wolves arranged an aeroplane to fly me there. By then Marion and I had a car and she drove me to Elmdon Airport in Birmingham as quickly as possible after lectures finished at 4pm. But what a shock we had when we saw the plane I was to fly in. It was tiny, almost like a toy model, with the propeller and cramped seating for the pilot and single passenger alongside him. I think it belonged to one of the Wolves' club directors and I was told later the plane had done reconnaissance work in the 1914-18 World War.

Marion was determined I was not to get into this death-trap! But I went. I'm not sure what navigational aids the plane had, but when we set off, despite Marion's unease, the pilot appeared simply to be following the railway and main roads. As the plane approached Sheffield, the pilot explained that he would be landing in a suitable field on the outskirts of the city where a Wolves official, George Noakes, the club's scout, would be waving a white towel to attract our attention and with his car engine running, ready to take me to the ground. Whether this landing had been authorised by the relevant authorities I never discovered, because the pilot, despite a lengthy search, failed to spot George's white towel and eventually we had to abandon hope of landing near Sheffield and flew to an airfield at Worksop to set down. Glad to be back on firm ground, I hitch-hiked a lift by car into Sheffield, reaching Bramall Lane about ten minutes before the final whistle. Wolves had taken a reserve with them I case I was not able to make it to the ground on time and the team were at this stage leading 2-0, but in those last few minutes Sheffield United scored twice, which meant Wolves finished third when a victory would have given us second place in the League Championship. When I went into the dressing room afterwards I did have a lot of leg pulling I can tell you!

I LOVED PLAYING at wing-half rather because you were involved in the game all the time and you weren't so dependent on other people. You just felt so involved and I enjoyed that. I think I had a good vision of the game. My use of the ball was good. But you couldn't play at the Wolves at that time and not be strong in the tackle or good at winning the ball. You had to be. But when you won it you also then had to be able to use it. We were known for one or two different reasons. We did play a racy style, getting it quickly out of defence to the wingers and following up swiftly to be available to take the game on further. That meant you were really busy and I was in the thick of it. The long ball tag that the newspapers gave us was simply because we looked to get the ball to our wingers because they were so fast and if the opposition were attacking it gave them more space. So the negative connotation of "long ball" really didn't apply. We scored a lot of goals as I said before and won the League Championship in both 1957/58 and 1958/59 and only missed out on a third consecutive title by a point the following season. There was compensation, however, in the form of the FA Cup. I had become captain of the club by then, after Billy Wright's retirement, and so after our 3-0 victory over Blackburn the pleasure of receiving the trophy fell to me. Prior to the Cup Final the Football Writers Association had voted me Player of the Year, and, although I was pleased to receive this recognition, it was in my view a tribute to the entire Wolves team following its achievements over the previous three seasons.

Our success was based on having a very good spirit in the club. None of the pros ever had a problem with me not training very often with them, but still being in the team. What mattered was winning football matches. This spirit also manifested itself in a steely determination in the way we played. We never felt beaten throughout that period. We were competitive and had a will to win and we enjoyed winning. We scored late goals on many occasions because of our fitness and our desire. Stan always used to say that games lasted the full 90 minutes. That proved to be the case in this most special match.

I HAD BEEN hugely impressed by the Hungarian team which won the Olympic football tournament in Helsinki in Finland in the summer of 1952. Participants in the Olympic Games at that time were supposedly amateurs, but in some countries such as Hungary and others from Eastern Europe, although competitors held positions in the Armed Forces or other public services, they were in effect full-time professionals, able to train and prepare for competitions as such. So this 'amateur' side of theirs which was actually the full international side contained great players such as Puskas, Hidegkuti and Groscis. Needless to say Britain did not do very well as we really were amateurs, although several of us had league experience!

Walter Winterbottom, who, as well as having just been appointed head coach to the England team by the FA, and was also coaching the Great Britain amateur team at the Games, invited me to write an article for the Football Association's *News Magazine* about the tournament and, especially, about the winning Hungarian team. In it I made reference to the wonderful ball control of the Hungarian players, the speed and accuracy of their shooting and passing, and the novel tactics at that time of giving centre-forward Hidegkuti freedom to take up deep positions behind the other forwards. This allowed the Hungarians to pull defences around. While the Hungary team had many outstanding players, I mentioned in particular Puskas who, in defiance of all the coaching manuals, controlled the ball, made and received passes and shot at goal only with his left foot

But there was little reaction to the article in England, In fact it was rather poo-pooed, saying, "Look. They are amateurs. They haven't been tested by playing professionals." Until that was, in November 1953 this same Hungarian team came over and walloped the full England side 6-3 at Wembley. Everything changed after that. The game was televised too, which made it all the worse. It sent shock waves through the entire footballing nation. No one expected to concede six goals at Wembley. Of course when we played Honved in December the following year, five of their side had been in that team which humiliated England.

Then, in May 1954, in the final warm up game for the World Cup in Switzerland, England suffered an even heavier defeat to Hungary, 7-1 in Budapest. Surprisingly Germany defeated Hungary in the final of that World Cup tournament. Actually the Germans were quite clever. The two countries met in one of the preliminary group matches and Germany, fielding a team mainly of reserves lost heavily, but still won their other two games to qualify. When both teams progressed through to the final, Germany, fielding a much stronger team than in the group match, won.

DURING THE EARLY 1950s, prior to the introduction of the European Cup and other international club competitions, Wolves arranged a number of so-called 'friendlies' against high-profile overseas teams under the new Molineux floodlights. Wolves were probably the most glamorous club in England alongside Manchester United, so this game of ours against Honved, the Hungarian champions, was now billed as the club championship of the world.

The previous friendlies had become something of a newspaper story as they liked to see them as England versus the rest of the world. These matches were a little bit special. I remember, for example, matches against Moscow Spartak, which Wolves won 4-0, and Dynamo Moscow, while we had beaten Maccabi Tel Aviv 10-0 two months before we faced Honved. One of the matches, played during the 1953/54 season, was against Racing Club of Buenos Aires. Although at the time substitutes were not permitted in English football, Wolves agreed that Racing could use them. But as the match progressed in the second half and we went several goals ahead, the opposing players seemed to be entering and leaving the field at an ever-increasing rate. At one stage I said to Billy Wright, "Do you know I think they've got more players than us," so we counted them and they had 12 players on the pitch. We drew this to the attention of the referee and there was a lengthy delay while the players argued about which one of them should leave the pitch. Then later in the game Arthur Ellis, the referee, awarded us a penalty and after Hancocks had put the ball down, one of their players kicked it off the spot. Then he did it again, delaying things further and the Racing manager walked on to the pitch. We thought he was coming on to restore order, but he just walked over and kicked the referee, who then just blew his whistle and ended the game. Next they went to play Coventry and that game was stopped at half-time!

The most important of these floodlit matches was, of course, the game against Honved in December 1954. Prior to this game Wolves had been unbeaten against visiting teams from abroad; but when it was announced that the next opponents would be Honved, the top club in Hungary, boasting many members of the national team which had defeated England, there were fears of another high-profile defeat for an English team. There had been almost a hysterical reaction to how Hungary had beaten England twice and the BBC were therefore televising the match as Wolves, of course, were reigning Football League champions. There was, however, a better mood generally in English football after the humiliation of the Hungarian defeats and failure at the quarter-final stage of the World Cup in Switzerland. England had recently beaten the world champions, West Germany, 3-1 at Wembley with Billy Wright and myself, winning my second cap, in the team.

OF COURSE THE floodlights were pretty new at that time which was the other thing which made these games so special. And in the winter evenings there used to be this eerie fog which descended on Molineux which also added to the atmosphere. The mere fact of a floodlit game made it an occasion for people. When the referee called for the teams, the Honved players walked on to the pitch in their smart tracksuits like a well-drilled military platoon, which was perhaps not surprising since they were the team of the Hungarian Armed Forces.

Wolves tried out some new satin shirts. They reflected the light and people thought they were fluorescent, particularly on TV, where the old-style cameras made us look like we glowed in an almost superhuman way. But these shirts did not absorb the perspiration of the players as the match proceeded and became increasingly uncomfortable. I gave my shirt away to one of the Hungarian players after the match and was pleased to be rid of it.

As the match got underway Billy Wright must have been thinking of England's two heavy defeats against Hungary, particularly one incident in the Wembley match where Puskas rolled the ball back under his left foot, leaving Billy on the floor as his tackle failed, before lashing the ball into the net, with his left foot again, of course. In this match either I or Ron Flowers marked Puskas depending on the position he was taking up. I found it helpful that I had seen and studied him in action, live and on television, during the 1952 Olympic Games, Hungary's two games against England and the 1954 World Cup.

Stan Cullis did not propose any particular tactics for the Wolves players before the Honved match. Hidegkuti was not a member of their team and there was no need to consider ways of combating his style of play as a deep-lying centre-forward behind the other forwards. Honved played with a more conventional method in attack, but it was still of very high quality.

The night before the match we had a civic reception for the Honved travelling party and in his speech the Mayor of Wolverhampton reminded the Hungarians that thus far no visiting European side had managed to score at Molineux. Of course that kind of tempting fate was tantamount to handing Honved an early goal. In fact it was worse than that as they scored *twice* early on. The first came from a free kick which was headed in and then, just a minute later, Roy Swinbourne was put clean through. The Honved goalkeeper saved at his feet, though, and instituted a quick counter-attack. Honved swept straight down to our end and their centre-forward, Machos, was put clean through. He ran past me on to the pass and I was directly behind him as he ran in on the Wolves goal. His shot was very well placed and Bert Williams had no chance of saving it. As soon as Machos let it go I thought "Gosh. It's there." The speed with which Honved had turned defence into attack, suddenly giving them a 2-0 lead, had to be admired.

Apart from the two goals, there were other reminders in the first half of the match of the high quality of the Honved team's play, particularly that of its forwards. They were wonderful artists with the ball. They passed the ball well. Although I don't think they played with quite the same fluidity as the Hungarian team. I was not aware of their full-backs being any better than ours. But they had marvellous attacking players, skilful inside-forwards and racy wingers. But Wolves also played well, creating a number of scoring opportunities. As we left the pitch at half-time, they believed strongly that Honved's 2-0 lead did not do them justice.

STAN CULLIS WAS calm and relaxed during half-time despite the two goal deficit and seemed confident that we would "come good" in the second half – which, of course, we did.

During the early stages of the second half, Wolves attacked strongly and when Johnny Hancocks was fouled in a scoring position we were awarded a penalty. There were one or two protests from the Honved defenders, but Johnny was Wolves' regular penalty-taker and was not put off by these and struck the ball hard into his favourite corner of the goal. Our tails were up now and we attacked constantly.

The ground was quite heavy due to the winter rain. It had also been watered and that really helped us as the Honved players got more and more bogged down and tired, while our fitness and determination helped us push on. Their passing deteriorated and Wolves frequently intercepted it, even in the Honved half of the pitch. That put pressure on them. Apparently they also had a particular dislike of playing in rain and the conditions got murkier and murkier as the game wore on, which really helped us.

We were also pretty fit. I wouldn't like to judge their fitness. But I mean Puskas himself didn't look that fit. He was obviously slightly chubby and he wasn't a worker in that sense, but he was a beautiful worker off the ball. I think we ran them out of the game, which was a feature of our play and something we did regularly in the First Division. We were very much a team and that ethic allowed us to keep powering on.

Eventually this advantage allowed us to score twice in close succession to clinch victory. Roy Swinbourne scored both of them, finishing off crosses from either wing. The winner was special, partly because it decided the game in our favour, but partly because Roy hooked a Les Smith cross from the left wing back over his shoulder in spectacular fashion to net.

We received tremendous applause as we left the pitch at the end of the match. I think the fact that we came back from 2-0 down added a touch of magic to that night and that's why it has become so legendary among supporters across the land. Once we got back to 2-2 our tails were up and we knew we were going to win.

There was plenty of applause too for Honved as they had played a huge part in a superb match. I swapped shirts at the end with Budai, the outside right, but I actually wasn't feeling awfully well. I had a cold coming on. I felt OK during the game, but felt awful afterwards. A banquet had been arranged for the two teams after the match, but I wasn't feeling well and not looking forward to the walk to Wolverhampton station and the train journey home. On hearing this, Stan Cullis arranged for a taxi to take me from Molineux all the way home, stressing that it wasn't usual for Wolves to make such arrangements for its players!

I imagine Billy Wright, after his experience of the internationals against Hungary, enjoyed a quiet satisfaction about the result, though he wasn't the sort of person to show this. He developed quite a lasting relationship with Puskas over the years and they became very friendly. Even after they had both retired as players, Puskas called on Billy whenever he visited England.

THE REACTION TO the game was exceptional. One newspaper headline referred to Wolves as "Champions of the World". That was a bit special. Had England not been beaten so soundly by Hungary I think the Wolves v Honved friendly would have been regarded more as an ordinary game. But in the circumstances it took on special significance. It was a matter of national pride and gave everyone a lift in the way only football can to the mood of the nation. I don't think I was particularly conscious of that myself. It was more of a national newspaper thing.

Apparently it was that headline which prompted a French journalist to set up a pan-European competition between the champion clubs from each country to find the best side in Europe – specifically to prove that Wolves, or any other English team, wasn't the best. The European Cup began the following season, so we can even claim to have been the spark behind that.

MALCOLM FINLAYSON: BORN 14 JUNE 1936, DUMBARTON; 179 GAMES, 0 GOALS

# Malcolm Finlayson

## Wolves 3 Real Madrid 2

### European friendly

### Thursday 17 October 1957

WHEN I JOINED Wolverhampton Wanderers from Millwall Football Club in 1956, the club fielded eight teams, four of which were professional. The club had developed this system of feeding through players from one team to the next, promoting those with first team potential at each grade and selling on or releasing others with less ability. Stan Cullis, a strict disciplinarian, also released those who stepped out of line.

From 1948 until about 1960 he managed to replace top players on a regular basis with others who were coming through to keep the momentum going. That was an incredible achievement and also, as Wolves were successful in the 1950s, any player brought in from another club was only too eager to sign, and I, who as a 12-year-old had seen and admired Stan Cullis captain England at Hampden Park, was no exception.

At 17 years of age in 1948 and playing for Glasgow junior side, Renfrew, I was spotted by a Millwall FC scout and invited down for a trial game. I signed, and ten days later made my debut against West Bromwich Albion.

Eight years and 251 games later for Millwall, whilst on the transfer list after a disagreement over a part-time job I wished to take, I was in Charlton Athletic's boardroom at midnight, talking to their manager, Jimmy Seed; and being invited to replace that flamboyant goalkeeper Sam Bartram, who had retired without a satisfactory replacement being found.

The next day I was instructed to report at Millwall and to my astonishment told that Ron Gray, their current manager, would accompany me to Molineux, not Charlton, as Wolverhampton Wanderers wished to sign me. Nigel Sims, Bert Williams' understudy, had been sold to Aston Villa, and Noel Dwyer, his understudy had broken his shoulder.

George Noakes, the Wolves chief scout, had seen me play in a particular game at Walsall some years before. Millwall were leading 1-0 when I received a nasty face injury, which necessitated several stitches, diving at the feet of a player called Johnny Devlin, and I was taken to the local hospital accompanied by an elderly Millwall director. By the time I returned; with our striker Jimmy Constantine in goal, we were 3-1 down, the gates were locked as I wasn't expected back, and our elderly director was shouting with frustration as he tried to climb the gate for us to gain entry. Eventually he succeeded. I hadn't really recovered enough to play on, but I did, and I proved that by wandering into the same goal that I had been defending in the first half. Of course now it was after half time and I was at the wrong end!

The game continued to be end to end and was locked at 5-5 when our forward Johnny Short scored in the last minute. From the kick-off Walsall surged forward and the ball hit our crossbar before flying into the crowd. That was it, game over!! So George Noakes had witnessed this incredible match and remembered it nearly a decade later, so he suggested to Stan Cullis, who had also seen me play for the RAF versus the Army at Molineux in 1953, that I could be the right replacement for Bert Williams. I know Stan never regretted the £2,500 he spent on me because he once gave a newspaper interview in which he called me "the best buy he ever made". Note - not the best player!

We had a mutual respect for each other. That's not saying we didn't have occasional differences of opinion, but the respect we had was huge. In fact Stan told me that he had recommended me to the Scottish selectors on several occasions, and he once told me that he'd been informed that I'd been selected to play against Wales at Cardiff; only to be mortified when someone else was chosen. The Scottish selectors, directors of the leading clubs and much influenced by the Scottish press, were reluctant to play 'Anglos' - their derogatory term, but especially those who had played all their careers in England without playing north of the border first.

In fact Dave Mackay, the Spurs and Scotland captain, always used to say that if Scotland lost it was always the 'Anglos' who were dropped first; even though that meant the likes of himself and Denis Law.

Speaking at a dinner in Glasgow, some years ago, I was asked if I ever regretted not being selected. I replied that if a choice had had to be made between Scotland and the Wolverhampton Wanderers team of the 1950s, which played and won against the European champions in those fantastic floodlit matches, and me being the only Wolves goalkeeper to date to hold two championship medals and an FA Cup winner's medal, that there would be no contest. Wolverhampton Wanderers would be my first choice.

I did not sit down to rapturous applause!

AS I WAS replacing the England keeper, Bert Williams, comparisons were bound to be made.

Bert, though smaller than me but more agile, could afford to position himself and then when an opponent shot at goal, used that agility to make a save. I, a lifelong disciple and of similar build to England keeper Frank Swift, attempted positions and angles whereby I either got out to the ball before the opponent could shoot, or alternatively position and spread myself at the right angle to block the shot. The former tactic, in what was then, but is no longer, a very physical game, resulted in two broken cheek-bones, one shoulder and numerous head stitches and broken fingers, as forwards would trample all over you in their efforts to get to the ball first. As charging the goalkeeper, when in possession, over the line, or in an attempt to dislodge the ball was legitimate then, I always stood my ground and met any shoulder charge robustly, as any other attitude would indicate weakness, and encourage the opposition.

Of course, all top teams had centre-forwards of the calibre of West Bromwich Albion's Derek Kevan, Tottenham's Bobby Smith, Arsenal's Cliff Holton etc. All 6ft tall and built like brick outhouses! At least that's what it felt like when they shoulder charged. It made for some interesting exchanges, but at the final whistle everybody still shook hands, as there was always mutual respect!

The doyen of them all, Bolton's Nat Lofthouse, rightly named 'The Lion of Vienna' after almost single-handedly winning a game for England against Austria, was the hardest physical challenger, never losing an opportunity to try charging you over the goal line. He was superb both in the air and on the ground. I always thought he'd come off best charging at a brick wall! He had this fearsome reputation, but there was never an occasion when we didn't shake hands after a game. I saw him at a Wolves dinner some time ago and he said to me "wasn't it great then!" I don't think you get that sort of camaraderie between players these days.

One mistake I made, which fortunately didn't cost us the game, happened at Manchester City. Roy Paul, their captain and Welsh international wing-half, hit this free kick from about 30 yards out on the sideline. I expected him to hit the ball to the far post where his forwards would arrive to connect with it, so moved out to cover it. But Paul mishit the free kick into the centre of the goal, and because I'd already started to go, I was off balance and struggled to get back. I got there, but off balance and jammed the ball against the underside of the bar with my finger-tips. Their centre-forward Billy McAdam came in and hit me and the ball into the net! Goal!

At the top level a manager has to have confidence in his keeper and he, in turn, has not only to be consistent, but capable at times of unexpected saves which keep your side in the game. That happened in the 1960 FA Cup Final against Blackburn Rovers. At 0-0 their forward Peter Dobing was clean through, but I saved at point blank range to keep the score even. We were conscious that if that had counted, we would have needed at least two goals to win, a mountain to climb in an FA Cup Final! We eventually did win 3-0.

Because of the physical challenges involved from opponents, I learned early in my career to kick with both feet and continued with this practice all through my career. After normal training I would go down to Castlecroft taking two groundstaff boys with me to retrieve the balls and just kick endlessly with both feet. I also trained in the small gym pen under the stand by having someone kick the ball off the wall. Then I had to stop it at whatever height and angle it came at me. That helped my agility. So did all the skipping that I did to keep me literally on my toes.

I always thought that diving should be the last resort for a keeper. If you move your feet quickly enough you can get close to any ball. Another training routine I picked up and adapted was using a punchball to practise timing my clearing punches for crosses which could not be held. I became like a boxer, I had to really, because I wouldn't afford to mispunch in our own goalmouth.

I also learned at an early age that the goalkeeper is the only player facing the play, who sees the whole picture and therefore can instruct his defence. For instance, when unseen opponents are moving on the blind side of defenders etc. Essentially therefore, he would command the whole 18-yard box and, at times, beyond.

WOLVES' TRADITION OF floodlit friendlies was well established by the time I joined the club. The great nights of playing Moscow Dynamo, Spartak and Honved had already entered into a sort of folklore and of course nowadays, because they are that much further away in the past, they have become legendary. But when we heard that we would be facing Real Madrid, that for me was an exciting challenge. Madrid had won the first two European Cups and so were clearly the best club side on the continent. Of course no English club had entered the first competition because Alan Hardaker, the league secretary, was very against it, seeing it as a distraction. Madrid had defeated English champions Manchester United in the second competition at the semi-final stage, so we knew we were playing a good team.

We were confident though. We knew *we* had a good team, despite the couple of changes which had been made recently. Bill Shorthouse, one of the hardest men in the game, had retired in the summer of 1956, while we had also lost Roy Swinbourne with a debilitating injury and Johnny Hancocks had not long departed too. Losses like that could cripple sides, but Cullis drafted in players who were equally as good. .In this case Gerry Harris, Jimmy Murray and Norman Deeley. .I suppose you could say the same went for me when I replaced Bert Williams. This revamped side would go on to win the league for successive seasons, then win the FA Cup in the following campaign and miss out on a third consecutive title by one point.

There was this mystique about foreign opposition in those days as no one had seen them play much. It's not like the modern era where you see highlights of every Champions

League match. European competition was in its infancy and we hardly knew anything about some clubs. I remember going to play Red Star Belgrade in the European Cup in 1959 and Stan hadn't been able to send anyone out to watch them play. So when we arrived there we had a team meeting in a very austere room in our equally austere hotel and Stan asked a British diplomat from the embassy to come in and tell us about the team. This guy came in and told us how the goalkeeper was a cat and saved everything, the full-backs were brick outhouses and the forwards could score goals at will. Stan listened and then said ironically, "I don't know why we've bothered to come then! Now I'll tell you what we are going to do!" We drew 1-1 in Belgrade and won 3-0 at Molineux in the return!

ANYWAY WHEN WE played Madrid, Wolves had actually installed a new and improved set of floodlights in the summer. They were higher than the previous ones and boasted many more lamps. We'd beaten Spurs 4-0 in the first game played under them just a few weeks before we met Madrid.

The day before the game we had a light training session and a team talk. Stan never usually said much on these occasions, but I remember him saying, "Catch the bus early won't you." He was concerned about how we'd manage to get through the crowds flocking in to see us take on these Spanish champions. I don't think any of us had the benefit of a car then. Well you couldn't really on £20 per week!

Billy Wright didn't play in the match because he was due to captain England against Wales two days later, so George Showell filled in for him. George often deputised for Billy and eventually he succeeded him when he retired a couple of years later. George then moved back to right-back before Eddie Stuart left to go to Stoke and Bill Slater wore the No.

5 shirt. Amazingly Gerry Harris had played the night before for the England under-23s, so heaven knows how he felt as he got changed for this game.

What carried us through so many games was that we trained so hard and we were powerful and fit. We were a popular side. When we played in London the gates at Tottenham, Arsenal and Chelsea were invariably closed at 2pm with up to 70,000 spectators inside.

Stan usually had the pitch watered, so the ball and pitch got progressively heavier. Remember this wasn't the plastic ball that is used today, which you could probably kick to Villa Park and back. The ball we used was leather and soaked up the water. It was doubly significant that night as Madrid were a team of ball artists, used to the hard pitches of Spain. They boasted the likes of Raymond Kopa, Paco Gento and Alfredo Di Stefano in their side. They were truly skilful players, but our plan was not to give them time to play.

Stan was always very good at assessing an opposing side's weaknesses. He didn't dwell on them, just pointed them out. Mostly his brief team talks focussed on what *we* were going to do. Not the opposition. We were essentially a counter-attacking team, at our most dangerous hitting teams on the break with our pace and with dangerous wingers creating chances when the opposition had fewer men in their own half. Often we sat back and then pumped long balls into the spaces for the wingers to run on to and fast, strong forwards to take advantage.

However, I remember once we were losing at half-time and we hadn't been playing particularly well, because, in Stan's opinion, we'd tried to play too pretty football. Stan sat us down and said forcefully, "You - You're playing like England players"! That wasn't a compliment. What he meant was that we were giving far too many short passes. He wanted us to play the ball forward early as we usually did.

I recall another fairly tense half-time dressing room chat in our championship year 1957/58. We were losing badly at Chelsea and Stan turned to the three half-backs and said ironically, "Tell me gentlemen, We've been playing for 45 minutes. When do you think one of you might get around to tackling their inside-left?" As it happens, that was Jimmy Greaves.

ANYWAY THE REASON I've remembered this Madrid match is simply that they were then the best. They had beaten all comers in the previous two seasons. I was proud to play against them and we admired them and their achievements. And of course, we were expected to beat them, as Moscow Dynamo, Spartak and Honved before them. Our crowd were probably the only people who thought we could do it. They'd seen us play so well and win so many matches that they probably thought it was a bit of a right of theirs to win. In fact they were very demanding. They once booed us off because we only drew at home to Arsenal. That was at Easter and was the first point we'd dropped at home all season!

On this night against Madrid the game didn't start so well for us, as the Spaniards scored halfway through the first half. We'd already missed a great chance when Jimmy Mullen went clean through on their goalkeeper, but missed. Madrid played well at the start and put us under pressure, and from a corner their inside-forward Marsal leapt powerfully to head the ball in.

I remembered thinking how good Madrid were in that first half. They were a passing team, hugely talented and their passes found their men like magnets attracted to each other. They were clever too. Raymond Kopa was very skilful and Gento on the other wing could run like an express train.

But I also played a part in the equaliser against Madrid early in the second half. It was a classic Wolves goal. I collected the ball from a Madrid attack and, spotting the gaps in their defence, pumped it downfield almost to the edge of their penalty area, where Jimmy Murray headed it on and Peter Broadbent raced through to lob over the keeper. Half of their team was still in our half when the ball hit the back of the net.

Jimmy was a cracking player for us. He had two good feet and could head a ball well. He wasn't as physical as his predecessor, Roy Swinbourne. In fact he was quite slight really. He was very clever at positioning himself to receive the ball in gaps and with Norman Deeley and Peter Broadbent around you just knew he was going to be found. Once Peter got the ball he always seemed to have half an hour to play it as he'd found space.

I remember once we were on tour in South Africa and beat Southern Transvaal 5-2 and Jimmy Murray scored all five. The national newspaper had this headline which said "Hail to the greatest football machine to visit South Africa in post war years" That was quite a compliment.

Anyway Stan Cullis always said that Di Stefano had the best balance he'd ever seen. He seemed to skate over the surface, no matter what condition it was in. Despite being fairly shackled by George Showell that night he did manage to release Marsal, who cracked a bullet of a drive past me with 20 minutes to go. That equalised our second goal which had arrived on the hour when one of our corner routines paid off at the other end. Norman Deeley floated the ball in and Jimmy Murray got up to head home. Then about 20 minutes later the ball pinged around the box from another corner and Dennis Wilshaw pounced, hooking the ball left-footed at shoulder height past the goalkeeper and into the net for the winning goal.

WE'D BEATEN REAL Madrid and from their point of view that wasn't supposed to happen! They were embarrassed and hastily arranged a return match two months later on 11th December. It rained for 24 hours in Madrid before we played and that really suited us. It was like having the Molineux pitch watered! It was a real quagmire.

The night before the game we had a banquet which was attended by lots of local dignitaries and politicians and what have you. We always had ours at the Victoria Hotel in Wolverhampton and it couldn't have contrasted more with the opulent surroundings we found ourselves in over in Madrid. The Victoria was such a bleak place we always thought it was worth a goal start to us!

The Bernabeu Stadium was only about five-years-old then. Their famous president Santiago Bernabeu had a great vision of the club, which certainly came true during those halcyon days and that really has extended into the modern era with the Galacticos that play there today.

The game started with a bit of a bang when Gento nearly scored with a pre-planned move straight from the kick-off. His shot hit the post thankfully, but we were warned and switched on right from the start. I think Eddie Stuart gave Gento an "enthusiastic tackle" just to let him know that he shouldn't be trying that sort of thing.

We played a bit more of an offside game against them and Stan had drilled us like guardsmen. That compacted the play and Madrid found it difficult to break us down. It was significant because one of their goals was actually offside.

We had already gone ahead by that stage when Bobby Mason put us in front with a header from a Jimmy Mullen cross about half an hour in. The offside goal came when Mateos was allowed to shoot past me when he was miles ahead of the last defender. It shouldn't have stood, but there's nothing you can do in situations like that.

My big moment came when they managed to legitimately break the offside trap by Di Stefano carrying it through himself. He broke clear and I came out to face him. He feinted to go to his left and I followed. Then he went to his right and beat me, so I caught his ankle and toppled him up. Now Alfredo Di Stefano was a total gentleman, like Stanley Matthews and Tom Finney. I'm not. I deliberately upended him. But Di Stefano was so frustrated that he kicked out at me and instead of giving the penalty the French referee awarded a free kick against him!

Di Stefano had the last laugh, though, as he did manage to score with about 20 minutes to go. He raced on to Kopa's pass to slot home. But their lead didn't last long as one of their defenders managed to lash a Mullen cross into his own net in trying to clear. That was as a direct result of our style of play. We often had teams running back towards their own goal and we managed to score quite a few that way. There was one in the 1960 FA Cup Final, of course.

We actually should have won in Madrid as well. Remember, no British team managed to do that until Arsenal in 2006. In the very last minute Jimmy Mullen whacked this shot and as it flew towards goal I thought "Oh we're going to nick it here!" But it hit the bar and we ended up settling for an honourable draw. Madrid hadn't been beaten at home in any competition for around five years and they were very proud of that record. They were lucky to keep it intact that night. I was proud to be part of a team which had caused Real Madrid so many problems. Of course these days no one cares about club friendlies, so I suppose it's difficult to understand how much this meant to us and our supporters.

We must have impressed the Madrid team as well as Alfredo Di Stefano made himself very unpopular in Catalonia by saying that we would run all over Barcelona in the European Cup when we were drawn against them in the 1960 quarter-final.

WE CELEBRATED AFTER the game, which was unusual for us and shows you how we felt about it. We actually went out on the town until five or six in the morning. Around that time, my room-mate Billy Wright and I got back to the hotel having spent our last few pesetas on a taxi back. For once Stan was very forgiving about all the partying.

After all, we had beaten the champions of Europe and that simply wasn't supposed to happen. In theory I suppose that made *us* European champions. Tongue in cheek, we can claim that right! Remember, as well, that they continued to dominate Europe for several seasons to come. They played that magnificent final against Frankfurt at Hampden in 1960 when they won 7-3. So we had done incredibly well.

That Christmas Wolves sent out a Christmas card as usual, but on this occasion it had a scene from the first match with me saving from Di Stefano. I value that as a memento of two memorable matches among the 233 appearances which I made for Wolverhampton Wanderers between 1956 and 1963.

RON FLOWERS: BORN 28 JULY 1934, DONCASTER; 512 GAMES, 37 GOALS

# Ron Flowers

## Wolves 2 Preston North End 0
## League Division One
## Saturday 29 April 1958

I DIDN'T KNOW what to call Billy Wright when I first met him. Should I call him "Sir"? It made me nervous just being around him at first. In the end he helped me out by just asking me to call him "Bill". Using the same dressing room as the likes of Pye, Hancocks, Mullen and Williams was incredible. My feet didn't touch the ground for weeks after joining up with the first team squad at Wolves, as I was floating on air. Jimmy Mullen was detailed to look after me. He enjoyed having me under his wing and making sure I knew what the drill was and that I integrated with the first team squad.

I think that was all due to Stan Cullis and Joe Gardiner, who ensured that there were no stars at the club. No egos. Everyone was down to earth with no airs and graces. They were wonderful times.

FROM AROUND 12 years of age I played for the school team. I followed in the footsteps of my brother, George. I say followed in the footsteps. He was the clever one – head boy he was. I was only ever interested in football. My uncle George (my brother was named after him) had played for Doncaster and Tranmere. All I ever wanted to do was play.

I represented my school team, the county and then England schoolboys. Alan Finney, a winger who later played for Sheffield Wednesday, was in the same Yorkshire Schools team. Alan signed for Wednesday at 15 and they wanted me to sign too, but my father was determined that I learnt a trade, so I decided to become an apprentice electrician on the railways. Then Doncaster Rovers came in. The great Peter Doherty was their manager, and persuaded me to sign as an amateur. Dad agreed to that as it didn't interfere with my apprenticeship. But after three or four months I hadn't played for Doncaster as there was no youth team or anything, just reserves and first team.

All of a sudden Wolves created this nursery side at Wath, which was only about five miles away from our village. And the manager there, Mark Crook, said to me, "Come and play for us in the Northern Intermediate League." So I joined them and played more football. We faced the likes of Newcastle and Sunderland's juniors. I had always been an inside-forward up to that point, but Mark Crook turned me into a half-back. I remember him playing me at left-half for the first time at Rotherham. Initially it was because he had a triallist to look at who was an inside-forward, but it just seemed to click. I was strong, big for my age, determined and I enjoyed tackling. I would also be marking an inside-forward, so having been one I had an inkling about what they were trying to do, which helped me anticipate their next move and bought me vital seconds.

Then, at the end of that season, Mark told us that Mr Cullis was coming up to see the team play. Well, of course, that meant everyone was desperate to perform well in that game. After the match Mr Cullis asked to speak to my father. I couldn't believe it. And Stan asked if I could be allowed to come to Wolverhampton to play one 'A' team game as a trial. So it was all arranged. Straight after that match I was offered pro terms, even though I wasn't quite 17 then. That meant I needed parental permission to sign. My Dad was determined that I'd finished my apprenticeship and I had to fight to get him to agree. Wolves offered me the maximum wage they could at that age, £7 in the season and £6 in the close season. I gradually persuaded my father to allow me to go and play football for Wolves. Eventually he agreed; although he made sure I knew what I was getting myself into. "Oh, alright then," he said. "Don't you come back to me and say 'I wish I'd stopped on the railway.'" He gave me lots of encouragement to do well, but he made me sweat over joining Wolves.

FROM THERE I progressed through the various levels of teams at the Wolves. I was in digs with Pete Broadbent until we both went to do our National Service aged 18.

George Noakes, the chief scout, told me to apply to be a physical training instructor in the RAF and I was based at Hednesford and then Cosford, which weren't far away and allowed me to get back to Molineux to play regularly. I remember seeing the commanding officer of Cosford in the directors' box on many occasions, so I think it's fair to say that Wolves had things organised to enable us youngsters to be available whenever possible!

I remember my debut. The sergeant came into the billet early on Thursday morning and said, "Flowers! Get up. Get down to Molineux now." When I arrived Joe Gardiner told me that I was in the first team. I remember the sergeant got tickets for that game as well! It was against Blackpool, who had the best forward line in the country with Matthews, Mortensen and Perry in their line-up. Cullis was cunning that day because Bill Shorthouse was injured, which was why I was in the team, and he gave me the No. 5 shirt as though I would be a straight replacement for him at centre-half. But Stan said to me to wait until after kick-off and then swap with Billy Wright to move to half-back. It didn't work. We lost 5-2, but I scored on my debut. The goal came from a corner, which I headed in. That was fantastic.

After we'd come out of the Forces, Pete and I were both regularly knocking on the door of the first team in the 1952/53 season. It was amazing being involved in the first team squad at this young age. I filled in along the half-back line in a Wolves team which missed out on the league title by a mere three points.

On a match day Pete and I would walk along the alleyway from our Whitmore Reans digs towards the ground with all the supporters chatting with them. It was about a mile's walk, with people asking us, "What do you think we'll do?" And we'd say, "We'll try for you." And then after the match they'd tell you who had won around the country. Often that was the first we'd heard of the results. Times have changed a lot.

I MANAGED TO make 15 appearances in the championship winning side in 1953/54, enough to earn me a medal. Stan Cullis eventually accommodated me more permanently by moving Bill Shorthouse to full-back and Billy Wright across to centre-half, so the half-back line was Slater, Wright and Flowers. We became fixtures in the team. Shortly afterwards I should have made my England debut.

Arthur Oakley, one of the Wolves directors who was on the international selectors committee, came to me as I was getting changed for a match at Burnley and said, "You're in on Saturday." England were due to play Scotland at Wembley. Anyway during the game I got clobbered by an elbow which broke my nose and gave me a clot of blood on the brain and meant I was nowhere near fit enough to play for England. I couldn't move for a bit afterwards. I couldn't even get up to go to the toilet on my own, because the doctor thought if he let me move I'd walk out of the hospital and join in training or something silly like that. I wish I had played as England won 7-2! What a game that would have been to play in.

At the time there was only one player in history who had won a Championship medal, an FA Cup medal and an England cap before he was 21. That was Cliff Bastin. My Dad was keen that I achieved that.

I already had the league medal, but funnily enough we really should have won the FA Cup that year, but we got knocked out on an icy pitch at Sunderland in the quarter-final. We went down to ten men early on because Bill Shorthouse decided to put a heavy tackle in on Sunderland winger Billy Bingham in order to give himself an easy afternoon. Bill used to know which players he could do that to! Anyway he slid in on the snow and slipped, his feet went right up in the air and he cracked his head on the hard surface. Bang! It knocked him out and he couldn't continue. I remember him lying there with his eyes wide open, not blinking, lying in the snow. Joe Gardiner raced on and squeezed freezing cold water on to his face with his eyes open and he never even blinked. I thought he was dead! Bill couldn't continue and we ended up losing 2-0. Of course with no substitutes it meant we had ten men for most of the games and we couldn't hold on. I am convinced we would have walked the Cup that year. But it meant I missed out on my ambition.

I still had my first cap by the time I was 21. Two months before my birthday in fact, as I got picked for the next international against France in Paris in May and I was desperate to play, but I wasn't really fit enough. Duncan Edwards was also being tried at this time [he had made his debut in the previous match against Scotland], so there was obviously something of a policy towards youngsters. But I didn't do myself justice in Paris as I hadn't actually played for Wolves between being injured and selected again for

England, partly because the season had just ended. It was a bad decision on my part to play as England lost 1-0 and it took another three years before I was picked again. When I got into the side then, I played 47 consecutive games. That taught me a lesson.

ALL SUCCESSFUL SIDES never rely on just one or two players to score goals. You can look through our Wolves team and say, "Swinbourne could score, Broadbent could. Hancocks and Mullen would get you double figures a season." Look at Chelsea today. They can score through Lampard, Drogba, Crespo, Duff, Robben, Cole and Terry; goals from all over the team. We were the same. Also, the Wolves team in the 50s had such a great attitude. We always felt we were going to win and that's half the battle. We finished third in 1955/56 and fifth the following season. Manchester United won both those titles. They were the only side that we felt could match us over a season and the games between us and the "Busby Babes", as they were known, due to their youthful make-up took on an extra intensity.

Our style of play was straightforward and simple. We drove forward relentlessly. We didn't play square balls. Cullis would go daft at you if you played a ball square. He always wanted us to play forward as it kept the pressure on the opposition, even if it sometimes meant playing the ball into an area where there was no one. In fact one trick was, straight from the kick-off, to get the ball forward right down by the opposition's corner flag and send it out for a throw for them. That actually creates pressure on them straight away, when the game has only just started and they have to work the ball clear from a throw. We would then mark all their men heavily and let them struggle to get the ball clear. Often we would win it back high up the pitch and be able to create chances.

We often got criticised for long ball tactics. Cullis was not particularly interested in midfield, it's true. He simply split the field into three. In our defensive third he would tell us that only the opposition could score, so we had to get it out and forward quickly. In the opposition's defensive third only we could score and we had to keep the ball in there as much as possible. The middle third was simply for moving the ball forward into our attacking zone. It was that simple. Every player, whenever they got the ball, had to play it forward. We just used to pressurise teams. Cullis always deployed a target man, such as Roy Swinbourne or Jimmy Murray, who would bring everyone else into play, particularly the wingers.

The newspapers called us long ball merchants, but I remember West Ham, who were supposedly a team that play proper, cultured football, would do exactly the same thing. They would look to break forward quickly and then support. Bobby Moore's stock ball was into the channels for forwards to chase, so that they could get forward into your third of the field. That was no different to what we did.

Bolton get criticised for long ball tactics in the modern game, but when I've seen them they are quite entertaining. They are playing in a similar way to us, although without the wingers. Apparently Sam Allardyce, their manager, is a big fan of Stan Cullis. Interestingly Sam hails from Dudley, so probably grew up watching us play. I don't think that's a coincidence.

THE 1957/58 SEASON was a great season as it saw our new team blend together and storm to the title. Our summer tour to South Africa was a major reason for that. Wolves had toured there before and it had gone well for the club, so when we heard we were going to tour there it created a lot of excitement.

I'd got married in February 1957 and our tour was so good I said that if I hadn't, I would have stayed there. South Africa was a fantastic country. I would have loved to get myself a job and lay down roots there, but I would never have got my wife to join me. I had plenty of offers from local clubs. Not strictly legal, but it was lovely to know that I was wanted.

It was a great tour for me football-wise as well. We were out there for six weeks and it went fantastically well on all fronts. We scored lots of goals, I remember Jimmy Murray getting all five in one match we won 5-2. But it was most important for our team spirit, which built as we got closer over the six-week period. By the time we got back home we felt we were so far ahead of other clubs that had simply taken the summer off. Stan Cullis used the tour to shift the team around a bit. Harris, Finlayson, Deeley and Mason replaced Shorthouse, Williams, Hancocks and Wilshaw. It was quite a change, but we gelled together so well while we were away. That was the genius of Cullis, and how he kept it going for so long, that he could recycle the team and replace great players with more great players that he uncovered.

I remember one thing happening in South Africa. Towards the end of the tour a gentleman came from Mozambique and called at our hotel to ask us players if we would like to stop in his country on the way back home and play a match. He offered us £100 each to play, which was a lot of money at the time. We were very keen. But Cullis turned it down. He had arranged to stay on in South Africa and play another game against a local side; he wanted to sign a young winger called Des Horne. Somehow it fell to me to tackle Stan about this. I asked him if we were going to get anything extra for playing this additional game. He flew off the handle, saying, "Are you asking me for illegal payments? I'm going to report you to the FA. You wait until we get back to England." And I said, "Hey, hang on a minute. I was only asking." So that was the end of that.

OUR NEW TEAM got off to a fantastic start to the 1957/58 season. Our first two home games were 6-1 and 5-0 wins. Then we went 18 games without defeat from a 7 September loss at Luton to a Boxing Day 1-0 defeat at Spurs. Soon after that we had another fantastic run of nine wins from ten games. I think it was fairly obvious where the title was headed. Little Norman Deeley had been a revelation on the wing in place of Harry Hooper, who fell out of favour with Cullis.

Stan didn't suffer players who stepped out of line. It didn't matter whether they were good players. He always said, "Bad apples must leave the barrel." And he would always move players on to other clubs if he felt their behaviour was not in keeping with what he expected. Harry had breached club discipline in South Africa which meant he was shipped out and Norman given his chance. I know of two other players, who were in a similar position, that Stan simply sold. I'm not going to mention any names, but that was another incident on an earlier tour surrounding one of their birthdays. They broke Stan's disciplinary code and both left quickly afterwards.

Norman scored a hatful of goals that season. And I remember particularly him scoring twice as we defeated our closest rivals Manchester United 3-1 at home in September to take an important early lead in the title race. Norman ended up scoring 23 goals to finish as second highest scorer behind Jimmy Murray, who bagged 32. Norman's haul was not bad for a winger.

SOMETIMES WE RODE our luck. All teams who win things do. You can't win every game by five clear goals. When you play other good teams you have to battle to win and then sometimes you get lucky. We were rather lucky to win at Preston 2-1 in early December. North End subjected us to something of an assault and I remember Billy Wright marshalling his troops with a fantastic display of defending, popping up all over the place with all the sprightliness of a youngster, rather than his 33 years. Malcolm Finlayson also proved his worth in that game, bravely diving at forwards' feet as they broke through and bore down on goal. That was his style, and it often led to him being injured and whacked in the head. But he always got up and played on. That was the mark of our Wolves side. We were so desperate to win that we would play on through anything.

Our training helped us overcome teams. We used to do a lot of leg work to allow us to run on the heavy grounds of winter. Cullis wanted us to be as fit as we could be as he saw the benefit of being able to pressure teams in the last ten minutes of games, when they were wilting. Often we would score important goals in the dying moments of matches. It was one of our trademarks.

I'D ACTUALLY BEEN injured for some of the season, which meant I only played 28 league games. Funnily enough I picked up the knock in the last game of that 18-match unbeaten run against Everton and so missed the defeat at Spurs. But I didn't return until the Easter Monday win at Arsenal, the game which really clinched the title.

I say that win at Highbury really clinched the title, simply because, although Preston had a chance of winning the Championship when we met them at Molineux, they had to win this game, and their remaining three matches, while we had to lose all four of ours. It was an unlikely scenario; and also one which we could put a stop to right away by seeing them off in this game. In essence, though, this was a Championship decider because they were now the only club that could catch us and they *had* to win this game. It put us in mind to battle to the death to win the Championship.

Preston had emerged as our main rivals that season and were a fine team, boasting in Tom Finney one of the greatest players ever to live. They also had a great half-back in Tommy Docherty, who would later find fame as a manager of Chelsea and Manchester United. Then there was Willie Cunningham, a strong full-back who was built like a brick wall and felt like one when he tackled you too.

There was one strange thing about this title-deciding game though, which was that four of the biggest names in the two teams could not play in it!

Despite it being first versus second in late April, on the same day England were due to play Scotland at Hampden Park. This meant that we lost Billy Wright and Bill Slater, while Preston had Tom Finney and Tommy Docherty absent. How times have changed. Now clubs are forced to play vital games such as FA Cup quarter-finals during midweek to allow the national team to prepare for the 2006 World Cup. Back in those days there was no special treatment at all. You just lost your players and had to cover from within your squad for them.

I remember playing for England with Tom Finney, so I knew how much of a loss he was to Preston. We defenders used to say that if we were under pressure we could clear the ball out to Tom and he could hold on to it for five minutes before giving someone else a kick. He was that good! The Doc was another huge loss to them. He was a brash Scotsman, just the same as a player as he later became as a manager; always chatting away throughout a game.

So here we were facing up to each other without our international players, but I think it affected Preston more than it did us. Wolves had strength in depth. Cullis always ensured that. It was why he ended up with four England half-backs on his books once Eddie Clamp emerged as an international player at the end of that season.

The build up to the game was odd as well, as there was a bout of influenza in the camp. It badly affected Stan Cullis, who wasn't well enough to give any pre-match talk, not that he did much anyway as he liked to leave us to it on matchday. The weather was cloudy and threatened rain, although the pitch was OK, considering what a bog it could sometimes be at Molineux.

I remember in the first minute we forced a corner and the roar which greeted it was deafening. I thought to myself that the crowd were really backing us in this massive game and it spurred me on. We piled the pressure on, but couldn't convert any of our chances and you began to wonder if this would be our day. Early on Norman Deeley put a great cross in, but it eluded everyone when just a touch on it would have sent it in. Then Norman hit the bar from a chip which beat Else.

At this stage our dominance was such that Malcolm Finlayson had only touched the ball from back-passes. Even defenders got in on the act when Gerry Harris hit a cracker just inches over the top. I thought we were destined not to score, but then, just before half-time, Norman finally found the net with a right foot shot after taking the ball round the onrushing keeper. Magic.

We had total control of the game then and should have scored more. But also now it was my job to ensure we did not concede, by breaking up Preston's attacks. With Eddie and Gerry Harris behind me, I knew we had a fantastic defence. Preston did come into a bit in the second half, but we were never going to lose our grip on this game. It mattered too much. As it turned out Preston actually had a hand in both the goals we scored that day as their full-back, Joe Walton, had attempted a back-pass which Norman latched on to for the first, then left both him and Else on the ground before steering the ball home.

Then, just a minute from time, Gordon Milne found the back of his own net in trying to deal with Peter Broadbent's clever cross. That was that. 2-0 and one league title to the Wolves.

WHEN THE FINAL whistle sounded the crowd engulfed us on the pitch, shouting, "We want the team!" They ran on and patted us on the back, hundreds of them, all celebrating a second league title win. After we'd somehow managed to squeeze off the pitch we went back to the dressing rooms to put on our new club tracksuits with striped collars, which looked very natty. Then, to massive cheers, we were greeted by the Deputy Mayor of Wolverhampton, Mrs Ilsley, in the directors' box and Eddie Stuart, the stand-in captain in place of Billy Wright, said a few words through a microphone to the thousands of people who had gathered on the pitch to celebrate. As he spoke, I remember looking out over this teeming mass of faces, all smiling at our achievement. Eddie told them that Billy Wright was with us all in spirit, which went down very well with the locals who all hero-worshipped Billy, and rightly so. And there was an equally big cheer when the supporters discovered Wright's England had won 4-0 at Hampden Park. After Eddie's speech, the club's chairman, James Baker, stepped into the breach to say a few words on behalf of Stan Cullis, who wasn't well enough to speak.

There weren't particularly any big celebratory social events at Wolves under Stan. We'd have the occasional dinner to toast special things like Billy Wright's 100th cap or winning the league title, but Stan always thought that he could reduce any backbiting which may have existed between players and wives if he kept that kind of thing at a minimum. I'm not saying that this sort of thing went on, but Stan preferred prevention as a policy.

In fact all my social life revolved around Wolverhampton's cricket and hockey clubs, where I'd help with instructing their youngsters, on technique and general fitness. They were much more social arenas and we had a ball with the people associated with them.

Stan certainly would not allow the players to over-celebrate or let us get too big for our boots. I always remember that once when we played at Newcastle the home club sent in a crate of Newcastle Brown Ale for after the game; the brewery that made it was right next to the ground in those days. But Stan wouldn't have his players drinking, so he sent it back saying, "No, thanks. Orange juice, please."

Even when we were awarded our League Championship medals it would always be a simple ceremony involving the Mayor. No big celebration which could go to our heads. It was hard, but you knew what you could and couldn't do. And we understood that he kept this sort of thing low-key for a reason. It meant he had this enduring image of a strict disciplinarian, but he treated us well and, importantly, he treated us all the same. To Stan, Billy Wright was as important, or as able to be dressed down, as a youth team player. He was so good as a coach because he could tell you what you were doing wrong and how you could improve. And you listened to him, because he'd captained England.

Alf Ramsey was totally different in his approach to building a team. I remember Greavesie once asking Alf if he could go out for a drink after the match we were due to play that evening. Alf refused to let him go alone saying, "Greaves. You are here to play football. If you want a drink, we'll go together." And we congregated in the bar that night after the game and drank as a team. Alf didn't like cliques and individuals. He wanted the team ethic. That was his way of developing it.

AS I MENTIONED before, Manchester United were our major rivals at the time and the Munich air crash was a terrible incident which cost English football so much. What hurt me personally most was the death of Roger Byrne. Me and Roger roomed when we were together with England and we both had an interest in physiotherapy. He was taking a course in it and would always be on to me saying, "Ask me this or ask me the other." And we'd test each other from a book he had. I was quite close to him and it was so sad when I heard of his passing. And Duncan Edwards, of course. He was a special player; so confident. He was such a big lad, still developing into one of the giants of the game. We'd played together in the under-23s and were selected for our first full caps together, although I missed that game as I said.

When we did finally play United the title was already ours. We visited Old Trafford in the last week of the season. They'd won through to the Cup Final on a tidal wave of emotion, so I think they were saving themselves. Mind you, Cullis made a few changes to our side too with Bryn Jones at left-back and Nigel Sims in goal. A few players were given the opportunity of having the experience of playing at United without too much pressure on them. It worked too as we still won 4-0 and I scored the final goal. I also scored in the last game against Sheffield Wednesday, but we lost that one 2-1. It didn't matter because we finished five points clear of Preston in the end.

It's funny how the mind plays tricks on you about what went on all those years ago. I often don't remember things as well as supporters who come and talk to me about those great games. I tend to remember the good things and try and forget the goals we conceded and those I should have scored at the other end! Winning that league title was certainly something special and it began a run of success which would last for three golden seasons. Wolves was a special place to be in those days and I loved every minute.

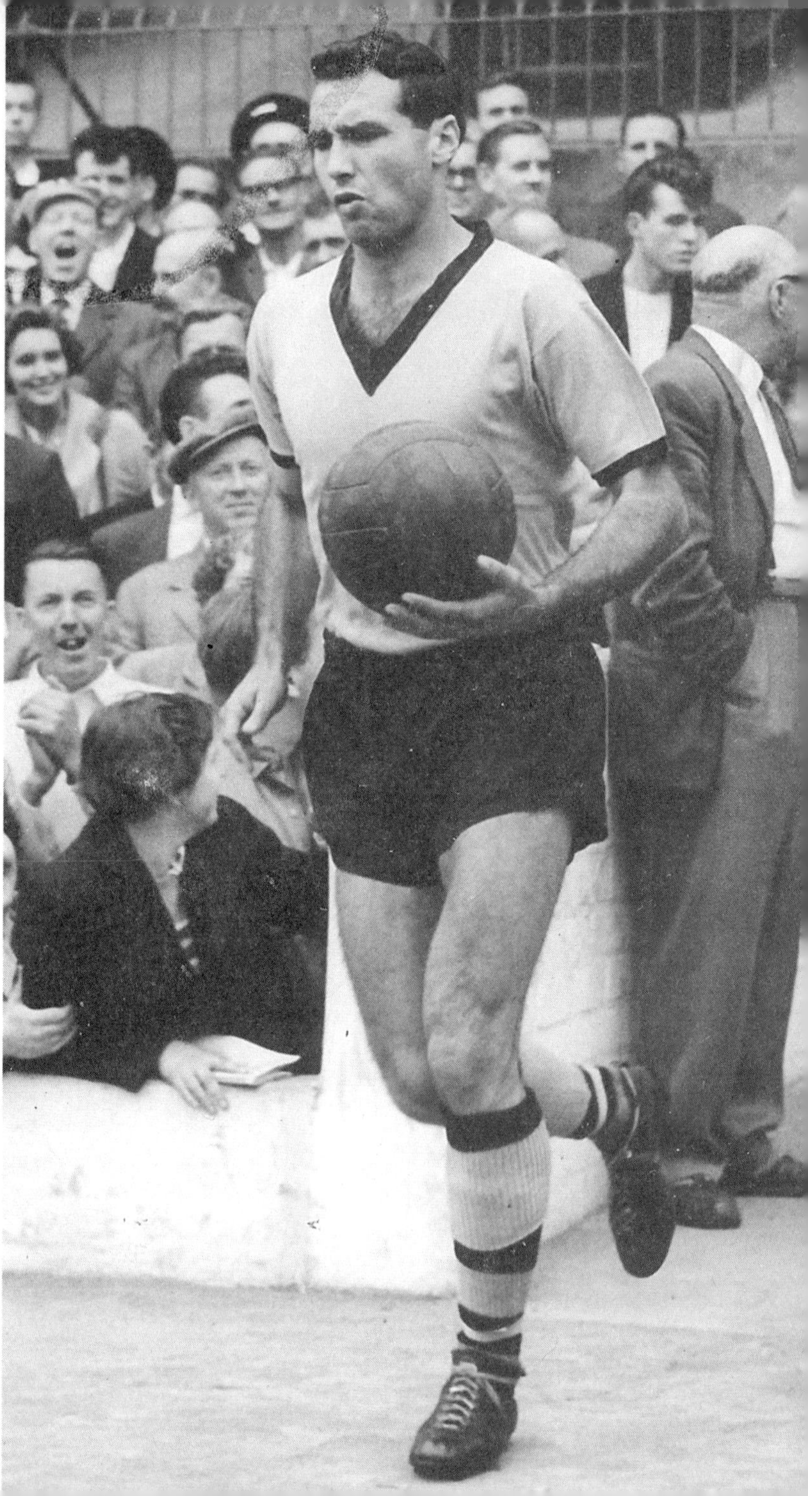

EDDIE STUART: BORN 12 MAY 1931, CAPE TOWN; 322 GAMES, 1 GOAL

# Eddie Stuart

## Wolves 9 Fulham 0

## League Division One

## Wednesday 16 September 1959

ON THE PITCH I was as hard as anybody in the world. You think some of the players today are hard? In my day we had some incredibly hard men playing the game and the tackling was fierce. Not dirty. We were strong; it was a man's game. I tell you, some of the players we played against were as tough as a brick wall. Jimmy Hagan, Jimmy Scoular, Harry Johnston. There was no diving or nastiness in trying to get each other sent off like you get today, though. It sickens me, that does. We played hard, but fair. The game was tough back then and you had to match your opponents or you would struggle to control the game. Wolves' style was to take charge, and that often broke teams mentally as well as physically. It worked. It must have done as we had plenty of silverware to show for it.

But we could play football too. I think there was a lot more skill around than today even. Take David Beckham, I actually wouldn't put him in the top 20 players in the modern game, because he's not particularly skilful at heading or using his left foot. But he has a wonderful right foot and this persona that's been carefully created for him. Back then there was none of that going on. We were down to earth. And I was proud to play for that Wolves team, proud to wear the shirt and proud to be captain. But it all could have been so different if I had taken another option about my future when I was a teenager.

BY THE TIME I was 16, I was 6ft and 12st 7lb. I was brought up in a religious family and one of my Aunts became a missionary and at that stage I was seriously considering becoming a church minister. But at the time I was playing for a team called Johannesburg Rangers in South Africa, which happened to be the same club that the great left winger Bill Perry played for, who later moved to Blackpool and scored the winning goal in the amazing 1953 FA Cup Final. I was the youngest player in the team and became the youngest player to play in the South African Cup Final.

We were the best team in the country and so attracted a lot of attention. A fellow called Billy Butler (former Bolton Wanderers player) came over from England to coach us. He also scouted for some English league clubs and spotted both Bill Perry and myself. Bill moved to England to join Blackpool at the end of that first season and I followed the next. Neither of us ended up at Bolton though. The reason I chose Wolves was because the club came to tour South Africa in the summer of 1951. I could have joined Aston Villa, but I thought Wolves were fabulous when they were in South Africa, so Wolves it was for me.

Within a year Bill Perry and I met again, except this time he was playing left-wing for Blackpool and I was right-back for Wolves and I was clobbering him of the pitch! "Nice to see you again, Bill!"

I actually had a jolly good job at the time, which went alongside playing football part-time. I worked for Barclays Bank in Jo'burg. I've always been very good with figures. Our family was very close and I don't think my mother really wanted me to go, but my father thought it was too good an opportunity to miss and I was very excited about playing in England, so off I went.

I'd just turned 19 when I came over to the UK. Gosh, I found it very, very strange. I arrived in January and the weather was appalling. I was travelling on the train from London via Coventry to Wolverhampton and it wound through some miserable areas as there was still lots of bomb-damaged housing from the war which had not been completely rebuilt and the landscape looked desolate. I thought "Crikey. What have I let myself in for?"

When I arrived in Wolverhampton, the chief scout, George Noakes, met me. He was a very nice man. He took me to my boarding house near Molineux and the landlady made me very welcome. The boat had stopped at Madeira on the way and I'd bought myself a lovely big box of chocolates. I always had a very sweet tooth and liked a chocolate or two. But being a well brought up boy, I offered one to my new landlady – and she took the lot! Of course in those days in England rationing was still in place and you were only allowed 2½oz of chocolate per week, which is why I'd bought myself a supply to keep me going. I could eat that much in a morning!

I met Cynthia, my wife, the second day of my stay in Wolverhampton. She was actually only 15 then and, although we struck up a bond straight away, because she was so young, dating was unconventional to say the least. Her father was Jack Lewis, the general manager of a co-op in the area.

I joined the Church of England at Tettenhall and at Codsall and taught Sunday School there. At that stage I had only just got into the reserves and so was only on £12 a week. I got a £100 signing-on fee, but my Dad took the £80 and I got to keep £20!

I WAS ALWAYS a right-back or centre-half, but I made my debut in the Wolves first team at centre-forward amid a bit of an injury crisis at the tail end of the 1951/52 season. I suppose I was selected because I was big and physical and could give and take a bit of stick. I did manage to score the goal that day, but we lost 4-1 to West Brom, which obviously was not ideal. As it turned out that was the only goal I ever scored for the Wolves, but I was glad to play in my more usual position the next few times I was selected.

Then something disturbing happened which almost had a profound effect on my life. I contracted an illness during the summer of 1952 when I'd returned home to celebrate my 21st birthday with my family and friends. Unfortunately, as I left South Africa to return to Wolverhampton I picked up some sort of tropical bug, which couldn't be diagnosed and found myself quite seriously ill. I did manage to return to England, but my condition was so bad that the club flew my mother over to be at my bedside. At first my career was feared for and then it got worse. I was actually given two hours to live at one point, but I think my fitness allowed me to fight off the infection, along with the best possible medical care which the club laid on and I actually got better very quickly, although I didn't make a first team appearance in 1952/53.

It wasn't until the 1953/54 season that I really sealed my place in the side. I'd made a dozen or so appearances in the Championship winning team the previous season as part of the crop of young players coming through alongside Ron Flowers, Norman Deeley and Eddie Clamp. But now I took over from John Short, who moved to Stoke, and made the right-back spot my own.

We players may have earned peanuts back then, but we were very famous. I remember the day Stan Cullis called me in at the end of the Championship winning season of 1953/54 and he said, "Eddie, you've now made 12 appearances for Wolves and so you can go into town and get yourself fitted for a club blazer." I was so delighted. I went straight into town and got myself this wonderful club blazer with the badge on the chest and I remember walking back through town and I felt 10ft tall. It's unbelievable isn't it? A simple thing like that and it meant the world to me. That was worth more than £20,000 a week. The recognition we got for our achievements was so important to me.

IT WAS ALWAYS an honour for me to be made captain of the team. I was stand-in skipper when Billy Wright was playing for England, which was actually quite a lot as in those days the clubs were not given the day off when the national team played. We had to cope without the likes of Billy, Bert Williams, Bill Slater and Ron Flowers, and later Eddie Clamp. Billy Wright was the most devoted man I have ever known and that was what made him so special at Wolves. He gave his *whole* life to Wolverhampton Wanderers in such a committed way, that he inspired all of us who had the honour of playing with him. He was always so reliable in defence and had an enormous leap for a relatively small man of 5ft 8in. He was a totally dedicated player and captain. Billy *was* Wolves.

My style as a captain was very different to Billy's. I would have a go at players if I felt they were not doing their utmost. I wasn't nasty, but I would have a go. I'd say, "You've got to do better. You're being paid and you're playing for Wolves. You've got that shirt on and it's very distinguished." But I could also help players as I was that sort of person. I had a lot of determination and I think that's why Stan made me captain in Billy's absence, to keep players on their toes. Actually I had a very good record, we hardly ever lost a match when I was captain and I took a lot of pride in that.

Being a defender at Wolves meant taking responsibility. Cullis would always tell you that as a defensive player it was your responsibility to defend and if you failed to cover because you were caught too far upfield and the opposition broke away and scored, then it was your fault and you would take the blame. He could be tough too. I remember he once came into the dressing room when we were losing at half-time and had a right go and I responded, which was a mistake. I said, "You don't know what you're bloody talking about," And he looked at me and thundered "Don't you ever say that to me again. I know more about football than anyone in the world. I'll see you in my office on Monday." And I tell you what, I had the most miserable weekend, I was dreading it! But I totally respected Stan Cullis as a person. I had the greatest respect for him. He was tough because he wanted to be the best and he demanded that you match his desire. I could relate to that.

Not all players could. There was one player, for example, who was a very talented player, but who, for some reason, never quite made the step up into being a fixture in the first team. One week he was playing in front of 50,000 at Molineux and next week in front of 50 at Halesowen in the reserves. That was how tough it could be playing for Stan Cullis and he ensured that players kept on their toes. Maybe he wasn't as determined as someone like me. You needed that kind of instinct to be consistently successful in football.

If we'd had a bad game we'd all make for the toilet to avoid Cullis' post-match wrath, but he was too canny to let us get away with that. He'd wait until we came out to make his points! He was such a successful manager because he was the master of situations like that. You could not get away with it. He had such authority. He commanded everything. At that time, after all, he was the most successful manager in football, so you really couldn't argue with him.

We used to play on the parking space outside the old main stand and sometimes Stan Cullis would join in. His control was fantastic. He used his arms well and shielded you off, he was a past master at that, having been captain of England in his time. But we'd often take the opportunity to kick him! Nothing serious, just a little nibble at his ankles. It was a tiny opportunity for revenge against him for dropping us.

In those days we weren't allowed to drive cars. Stan wouldn't let us. We had to go on the bus or walk to the ground. It was a club rule in case you had a mishap. He didn't want to take the risk. Billy Wright lived in the same road as me and we would travel to the games together on the bus. That meant that in all my years at Wolves I never paid a bus fare as I was travelling with the world famous Billy Wright. Because we lived so close together we would also go to the cinema together. And again we never paid because we were with Billy Wright. But the cinema manager knew what he was doing. With us being regulars there it encouraged many others to come along too, so the place was almost always full. Those were the kind of perks we got in those days.

I WAS AS fit as could be because we trained every day. But after training many players spent the afternoons playing snooker in the Molineux Hotel. But I wanted to do something more constructive with my life. So I went to work in an engineering firm in Bilston called Joseph Sankey's. With my experience in the bank in South Africa, I had a good head for figures and worked in the accounts department there.

Our team was packed full of great players. Billy Wright, Bill Slater, Ron Flowers, Eddie Clamp – four international half-backs for just three places in our club side. I have never known that in all my days. Peter Broadbent for example was a player before his time. He was an exceptional footballer, outstanding. His recent illness has come as a great sadness to us all and I think we saw what high regard he is held in by the turnout for the fund-raising dinner in February 2006.

BY THE LATE 50s we'd just built up so much confidence. We never felt we were going to lose. We always thought we could win any match and had no fear of any opponent. Our main rivals at the time were Manchester United, despite the Munich crash, which so cruelly robbed them of so many great players. I remember where I was when I heard that terrible news. Wolves were in Blackpool preparing to play United at Old Trafford on the Saturday afternoon. Billy Wright and I had gone into the town to eat at the restaurant in the Blackpool Tower itself and part way through the meal the head waiter came over and told Billy that there had been this terrible disaster. I remember that when we got on the tram to go back to the Northern Hotel, where we were staying, people were openly crying in distress. Of course that affected their club hugely, although I always believed that we would still have beaten them to the title in that 1957/58 season anyway as we were six points ahead of them at the time of the crash. But it was such a tragedy.

We retained the league title in 1958/59, by the margin of six points over United. We had an amazing run in the second half of the season when we only lost two of our last 21 games. We'd become a very efficient attacking machine by then too. I remember putting seven goals past Portsmouth, six past Arsenal and Leeds and five past Blackburn and Luton. We actually scored 110 goals that season, apparently that was the sixth highest total in top flight history at that point, and only since surpassed by Spurs. We had players all over the team who could find the back of the net regularly (except me!) and it was a joy to play in such an attack-minded side.

THE REASON I have chosen this match against Fulham was that I was captain of a team which won 9-0 in the top flight of British football. It was also special because we had actually lost 3-1 at Craven Cottage just a week earlier. That was our first defeat of the season and it had stung us because we were reigning champions and our pride dictated that we took this early opportunity for revenge. So we were determined to win. This was a midweek match and, even though it was very early in the season and the light lasted until late in the evening, the floodlights were on. At that time we felt that playing under the lights gave us something extra. We still had this incredible home record under floodlights against European teams. We'd never lost in seven years and had beaten the likes of Honved, Real Madrid, Spartak Moscow and Red Star Belgrade. We'd built up this reputation at Molineux, plus now we had won the championship two years in a row.

And what makes this game all the more important to me was that, because Billy Wright was playing for England the following day against Wales, I was captain of the team. I led them out. And then we scored nine goals. For me this game against Fulham just outstrips the biggest game of those European encounters, defeating Honved, winning 9-1 at Cardiff and several victories over West Brom, which were all special. But this game was just that bit magical because I was skipper.

I was very fast for a big man. That was one of my main strengths, along with my tackling, my physical strength and my heading of the ball, which often allowed me to play at centre-half as well as full-back. I did have one psychological problem to deal with. I always used to hate playing in shin pads. I always felt they slowed me down. In those days they weren't compulsory, so I didn't always wear them. I used to sneak them off as the bell went for us to go out on to the pitch and put them on top of the water container so no one would find them. Stan Cullis would have gone mad if he'd known. Then at half-time I'd come in and put them on again when he came in to talk to us. One day he inevitably caught me and he took me to one side and said, "Look, if you're going to behave like that I'll make someone else captain while Billy's away." So I stopped doing it then.

FULHAM HAD SOME big names in their side. Johnny Haynes (who'd actually been dropped by England and so was free to play against us), Jimmy Hill, Tony Macedo in goal. They were no pushovers as they'd shown in beating us the week before.

It was such a perfect performance. It could have been 15-0. They hardly ever came over the halfway line, so us defenders had nothing to do. I can't remember having much to cope with personally in terms of defending. It was a no contest really. Malcolm Finlayson had taken over in goal from Bert Williams by then. They were very different as goalkeepers. Bert had been so agile, whereas Malcolm was much bigger and stronger and had a very different style. But of course during this game he was barely called into play.

I remember Ron Flowers' goal the best because it was such a beauty. He took a pass and looked up and hit the ball perfectly from 40 yards, just ten yards inside the Wolves half. I mean he really drilled it. It arrowed right into the top corner with Fulham goalkeeper Tony Macedo standing watching in awe. It was a truly brilliant goal. Ron tells this great story about that goal to this day. About ten years later his son, Glen, went on holiday to South Africa. He stopped to fill up his hire car with petrol and the attendant at the station started to talk football with him. Glen, of course, mentioned that his father had played for Wolves and the attendant immediately said that the manager of the petrol station was Tony Macedo. So Glen went to meet him and introduce himself and Tony said straight away, "Your father scored this magnificent goal past me. Does he ever tell you about it?" "Tell me about it?" said Glen. "He never bloody stops!"

THE WOLVES SUPPORTERS reacted incredibly at the end of the game. They went wild. That kind of thing lives with you for the rest of your life. Just like those other amazing nights against Honved and Real Madrid.

I didn't sleep that night. I remember thinking "I'm glad Billy was playing for England." I was so pleased that I had been captain for something that might never be achieved again. It certainly hasn't been matched since. We'd beaten Cardiff 9-1 at Ninian Park, but this game was far more special being at home.

Actually, in the few days following the game I remember that some fans were actually a little disappointed that we hadn't scored ten. Despite the fact that this was the highest ever win at Molineux. That's how used to success Wolves fans were at that stage.

I think one of the things that also made this match sweet was that when we went to London we always felt the press and the clubs there would not acknowledge our success. None of them, West Ham, Spurs, Arsenal, Fulham, Chelsea. They would not admit that we were being so successful. And so to give one of those southern clubs such a sound beating also made us feel particularly good. Very pleased indeed.

THE BIGGEST TRAGEDY of my career was the way I was forced out of the team. On 21 March 1960 an event took place in South Africa, which has since become known as the Sharpeville Massacre. I don't know the ins and outs of exactly what happened, but I do know that a number of white guards shot dead nearly 100 black protestors. It was an horrific incident which raised the profile of apartheid around the world. Because I was from South Africa, somehow people got it into their heads that I had something to do with it or was to blame in some way.

There was a lot of coverage in the papers about Sharpeville and I had all these nasty calls. I had a shop, a general store, near the ground, and honestly we got these terribly nasty letters. I remember the next home game Wolves played was against Luton and I was captain once again. This time because Billy Wright had retired the previous summer. As I led the team out my own fans booed me. I was their captain. I'd given them nine years' good service and I'd played my guts out for them and I was very happy here and I loved Wolves, but here I was being booed by my own supporters. What went on in South Africa had nothing to do with me, but they treated me this way anyway.

The upshot of it was that after the game Stan Cullis, who was obviously well aware of what the reaction was, asked me to see him on the Monday morning. Then he told me that for the sake of harmony he would have to drop me. He was terribly upset. We talked it through, but I can understand why he had to take that decision.

That cost me and I believe it cost the club. I would have been the first foreign captain to lift the FA Cup at Wembley for example, but it allowed Bill Slater to skipper the team and lift the trophy that day. Before the final all the players came to me and shook my hand. It was terribly hard for me to take. I got a medal, Stan Cullis made sure of that, but it didn't mean a thing to me. Not a thing.

Without me Wolves actually went on a very good run in the league, winning ten of the last 14 games, so it's difficult to criticise, but I honestly think that I could have made a difference to the vital run in to that season. We lost 1-0 at Newcastle with four games to go and then, vitally, 3-1 at home to Spurs in the penultimate game of the season. Spurs finished third in the end and we finished second, one point behind champions Burnley.

I still feel we *should* have won the double that year. But you can't have everything in football. That's sport. There's always other teams opposing you, trying to beat you. And things happen. I don't blame Stan Cullis at all for what happened. He didn't have any choice. I just feel that it may well have cost the club a league title to go along with that FA Cup triumph.

Of course I managed to get my place back eventually and stayed for another couple of years, but eventually I moved on to Stoke, then Tranmere and Stockport. I was fortunate enough to be captain at all of those clubs and also win the titles of lower divisions, so I had a successful time, especially at Stoke where I helped the club, along with 50 year-old Stanley Matthews, back into the top flight.

But I look back at my time at Wolves with a real feeling of pleasure. Nothing beats success and we had plenty of it.

NORMAN DEELEY: BORN 30 NOVEMBER 1933, WEDNESBURY; 237 GAMES, 75 GOALS

# Norman Deeley

## Wolves 3 Blackburn Rovers 0
## FA Cup Final
## Saturday 7 May 1960

I WAS ONLY 4ft 10¾in when I left school, although I grew to a whopping 5ft 4½in eventually. But I was never worried about my height. I had bags of skill and plenty of pace and I knew I was a good enough footballer to be able to make it in the game. After all I'd played for England schoolboys at wing-half in a team containing Albert Quixall (Sheffield Wednesday), Ray Spencer (Aston Villa) and Bryan Brennan (Stockport), who would go on to have good careers in the game.

I'd played for South Staffordshire and the Birmingham and District representative teams and the Wolves' chief scout, George Noakes, came to see me when I left school at 15. He asked me to join the groundstaff at Molineux, but when he went to speak to my parents Dad initially said "no", because he wanted me to go to West Brom! But I wanted to go to the Wolves. I'd made my mind up and Dad agreed in the end. It was something special to sign the forms and become a Wolves player.

That was in 1948 and in the same intake were George Showell and Alan Hinton. Wolves won the FA Cup Final the following season, Stan Cullis' first season, so I knew I was in the right place. I was in the reserves by the age of 16. We won the Central League three years on the trot. The team was mostly made up of first teamers vying for a spot like Ray Chatham and Billy Baxter.

At this stage I was still a wing-half, but my lack of inches was beginning to be a problem playing there. The philosophy of the club was for us to be able to fill in at our position if an injury occurred in the team above us. Well that would mean me replacing Bill Crook or Billy Wright. I just didn't play in that style. Cullis brought me along slowly. I made my debut at Molineux in 1951. I marked Arsenal's Doug Lishman and we won 2-1, but of course Billy was back in the side the next week. I only made a few appearances and then I was called up to do my National Service when I reached 18.

I ENTERED THE South Staffs regiment and was allowed to play for Wolves if I got leave. Mostly I played for the reserves, but then we got posted to Balakinley in Ireland, by the Mountains of Mourne and later to Linden in Germany. I played in the Battalion team and really enjoyed it. I scored bags of goals thanks to my pace and shooting ability and really changed myself into a more attacking player. My game then was all about pace and passing, so perhaps it wasn't such a surprise that when I came back from serving in the Army I was converted into a forward. Stan and Joe Gardiner saw that they could use my pace on the wing and trained me to replace Johnny Hancocks, who was just coming to the end of his career. I was actually a tiny bit taller than Johnny, so I knew then there would be no barriers to me getting into the first team.

I was now 20 and I knew that I had to get my career moving again. I'd signed up to the Army Engineering Reserve to get an early discharge from National Service and that came back to bite me when I got called back because of the Suez crisis, which flared up in February 1956. I was taken out to Egypt and we had to work 12 hours on and 12 off stevedoring. Thankfully we weren't out there too long.

In the summer of 1956 Wolves went on a tour to South Africa when, incidentally, Stan signed outside-left Des Horne. That tour was brilliant for me. It really made my career. It went really well for me and I think it made Stan Cullis sit up and take notice.

I played 41 games in the 1957/58 season and scored 23 goals from outside-right. I was off. The team took off too. We won two consecutive titles and scored 100 goals three seasons in a row. We were a really good side and it was nice to play in that kind of football with those players. If one man was having an off day all the others rallied round to help him out. The dressing room was electric. I was always quite chirpy and loved cracking jokes. I'd do things like put freezing cold water in the bath after training!

One of the greatest things that Stan Cullis did to build that Wolves team was to sign Peter Broadbent. He spent £13,000 on him from Brentford in 1950. I'd actually played left-half against him at schoolboy level in the England trial in 1948 at Portsmouth when the South played the Midlands. He was only six months older than me, but he got a regular place in the Wolves side a few seasons before me. Now I formed a great partnership with him on the right hand side. We set up a pattern that only we knew. Often I would come inside and he would cross me and I would leave the ball for him to take on up the wing and then he would play me in with a reverse pass. His running off the ball like that was fantastic. Mind you, he wasn't bad on the ball either!

YOU ONLY GET out what you put in. It's a simple motto of mine, but over the years I've found it to be true. I trained so hard and put every possible effort into both my training and every second of every game and it paid off for me. We'd won two successive league titles and in 1960 we were in line for the double. We hadn't started well in the league – I remember losing 5-1 at Spurs and 4-1 at Burnley - but when Bill Slater returned to the side we kick-started a run which took us right into the title race. Our main rivals were Burnley and Spurs as it happens, so those defeats caused us big problems.

Our FA Cup campaign started well, though. We drew at Newcastle and won the replay easily 5-2. I scored in that game. The next round saw us see off Charlton, who were a Second Division side. We beat them 2-1. Then we had two away matches at Luton and Leicester. We won 4-1 and 2-1 respectively and got to the semi-final having played well, but without truly being tested.

STAN CULLIS WAS a hard taskmaster. He was like Manchester United manager Alex Ferguson in some ways. He would have a go at you to give you a kick up the rear. He was strict and hard, but to be successful you have to be. He had some strange ways of motivating you. Before the cup semi-final against Second Division Villa he called me into his office. I'd had a groin strain and I thought he wanted to find out if I was fully fit again, which I was. I sat down and he told me that he believed I had put some money on Villa winning the match. He was accusing me of gambling against us and planning to throw the match! He said he knew I'd been offered £500. I was shocked and I said, "Well, you'd better leave me out then, if you think that."

After that I went for a drink in the pub as I thought I wouldn't be playing the next day. I played dominoes and had a couple of bottles of beer, but when I went back to look at the team sheet that George Noakes always pinned up in the corridor on a Friday, I found that instead of dropping me, Stan had moved me from outside right to outside-left and dropped Des Horne. I think that was to motivate Des for the coming games as he was then scared he'd miss the final. As it happened Des had a great game at Wembley. Stan put me up against Villa's right-back, Stan Lynn, who was a rock hard defender and he knew I wouldn't be intimidated by him.

So, come the semi-final the next day at the Hawthorns, I was so determined to prove Stan wrong that I scored within 10 minutes and we held on to win 1-0. The next day I went into Molineux to get some treatment on my groin, which had flared up again a little bit during the game, and Stan was there. As I walked past him I said, "I threw the game then, didn't I?" I don't think he really believed I was going to throw the game at all. That was simply a way of motivating me to up my game in a big match. And you have to say it worked didn't it?!

The goal in that semi-final came because I was on the left wing actually. Jimmy Murray was put in down the inside-right channel and he shot across the goal. Nigel Sims, the Villa goalkeeper, who had until recently played for Wolves, parried the ball out. I always came in off the wing when I knew someone was going to shoot, so I could pick up the scraps and this time it fell perfectly for me and I smacked it in. No one had tracked me into the area.

The semi-final turned out to be our toughest game of the cup run. Villa played well and gave us a few scares. My groin pulled again just after the goal and I ended up as a bit of a passenger. I just tried to make a nuisance of myself on the left wing, but mostly the rest of the game was about us defending well. Malcolm played really well in goal. There were a couple of near things, but we hung on.

THE WAS QUITE a bit of controversy around the final. For the Wolves' part, Stan Cullis took the decision to drop Bobby Mason, who had played in every round of the Cup, in favour of young Barry Stobart. I can't tell you why particularly. In fact I don't think we'll ever know the reason why. It was just something Stan chose to do. Barry had only made something like five first team appearances prior to Wembley. We'd played at Chelsea in our final league match on the Saturday before the final and Barry was in the team. We won 5-1 which meant we finished our league programme on top of the table, one point ahead of Spurs and Burnley, who had one game still to play. Unfortunately for Bobby I think Stan thought Barry had played so well in that game he couldn't drop him.

By then we had lost the league title as Burnley had won their final match at Manchester City. It would have been three championships in a row of course, and the double too, because we then won the Cup, so we'd have beaten Spurs to the achievement of being the first 20th century team to manage that feat. But that's football.

Of course I was worried I'd miss the final with my injury, but actually that manipulation broke a blood clot up in my groin. The Wolves club doctor was called Dr Richmond. He used to stretch my leg around my neck – see it does help having a short body sometimes! He worked wonders on me and when he'd finished and I'd rested up I couldn't feel it at all.

WE WERE MASSIVE favourites for the final as Blackburn had only finished 17th in the First Division. Everyone expected us to win, but Wolves had been in this position before in 1939 when Stan Cullis had been in the team and so he did not allow us to consider anything other than that this would be a very tough match and we would have to go all out to win it.

On the Friday night before the game, we were all in bed by 11pm after having some tea and biccies! I had a couple of bottles of Double Diamond and they helped me sleep really well. When we got up for breakfast some of the players were complaining about not being able to sleep, but I'd had a wonderful rest! I remember the waitresses wishing us all the best for the game and then it was on to the bus for Wembley. I had a few butterflies as we drew up to the ground. I don't believe anyone can say that they don't get butterflies on a day like that. All along Wembley Way there were Wolves fans with scarves jumping up and down. They kept trying to jump and touch the coach's windows. We had to go so slowly down Wembley Way and I thought we'd never actually get there! We looked at each other then and said, "We can't lose this for them."

It's traditional to go and walk out on to the pitch before the FA Cup Final. We never really used to do that anywhere else. We were all wearing our club blazers, which we'd been measured up for at Lew Bloom's in Wolverhampton. But we walked around at Wembley and began to get ready about three quarters of an hour before kick-off so we weren't sitting around in the dressing rooms for too long. None of us were particularly superstitious and we had Bill Slater as our captain. He'd only just got back into the side and been part of our tremendous run which nearly saw us take the title. He'd been a great player, but was now coming to the end of his career. He made a great captain, though, after Billy Wright had retired. He wasn't one to go round geeing players up. His leadership was more on the field.

Then you get the knock on the door and it really is something different to walk down the tunnel at Wembley and into the light of the stadium. It's a long walk to the halfway line, so you have plenty of time to think, which sometimes gets to people. I remember, after shaking hands with the Duke of Gloucester, we broke away to warm up and when I put my ball down on to the pitch it actually ran away from me. The pitch was like glass. It just rolled away. I'd chosen to play in a medium stud, which was a good choice because the pitch was too hard to take a long one.

YOU DON'T TEND to settle down in the first five minutes or so. My stomach butterflies stopped after that and I felt much more with it, settled and concentrated. Blackburn did create one decent early chance when Peter Dobing went through on Malcolm Finlayson, but Malcolm saved at his feet and that turned out to be their only real chance. We started to play a bit then too. My job was always to get into the box from the right-hand side when the ball was on the left wing. It had worked the opposite way round for my goal which won the semi-final. Anyway, Barry Stobart made a good run down the left and got to the byline and whipped a cross in. I'd charged into the middle and Mick McGrath, the Rovers left-half, went with me. He actually got to the ball just before I did by stretching and sliding. With their keeper coming out to collect the cross I watched as the ball beat the keeper and rebounded off McGrath and into the net.

It didn't really matter as I would have scored anyway. Once the ball had beaten the goalkeeper, if Mick had missed it I was only a couple of yards behind him waiting to tap it in. But own goals are a nightmare to put behind you at the best of times and this one was in *the* biggest game of all. As it turned out that cost me a hat-trick in the FA Cup Final. If only you'd missed it, Mick! I'm sure you wish you had too. As I was racing in behind him ready to score I couldn't stop myself from following the ball into the net and clinging on to the rigging in celebration. I didn't normally celebrate too much, not like they do these days, but a goal at Wembley is special.

BLACKBURN WEREN'T WITHOUT a bit of controversy themselves, although we didn't know about it until after the game. It turned out that their star forward Derek Dougan, who of course later became well known to Wolves fans, had put in a transfer request the night before the game. That must have unsettled them quite a lot.

The controversy didn't stop during the game either. Obviously having lost the league like that we wanted to win all the more. Now we were a goal up our first thought was to defend the lead and so we made sure we won every tackle we could. It was around then that the incident the game is now most famous for happened. The ball was knocked out towards me as I ran inside off my wing. It was a bit short and so tempted Blackburn full-back Dave Whelan into the tackle. I might only be small, but I could tackle as well as any Wolves player, because I'd started out as a half-back. Dave and I went for this ball and we arrived at speed pretty much together. Crunch. I heard this crack as we collided and I thought "That's my leg." When I looked down in my dazed state there was a duck-egg shaped bump already forming on my shin. Then I looked across at Dave's leg and there was no flesh on it for about four or five inches. He barely moved and it was obvious straight away he had done something bad. It was a really awful incident and in a way it still overshadows the success we had in the Cup Final to this day.

Dave was carried off and it turned out that his leg was so badly broken it ended his career. My leg was sore, but I could jog on it. It certainly didn't help Blackburn as, playing against ten men, we just kept the ball and tried to work openings. That huge pitch took its toll on them as they chased us around. There'd been this succession of injuries in Wembley finals which had started a debate about substitutes. It was known as "the Wembley Hoodoo". We hadn't given it a thought.

But it didn't necessarily help us either. Sometimes ten men play just as well as 11 as they try so hard to make up for the loss of a body. We didn't find it easy, but all the same we didn't find it too much of a problem. Still with only a goal lead, we couldn't be complacent.

AS WE WALKED off the pitch after the half-time whistle, BBC TV asked me if it was actually my goal. Live on air, at half-time! I told the nation that Mick had scored it. I could have claimed the goal then and I would have had my hat-trick, but I knew Mick had got the touch not me and I thought it was obvious. I also didn't know what destiny had in store for me in the second half.

When we got into the dressing room all Stan said to us was "keep going". I saw him change his shirt as the one he was wearing was wringing with sweat. It was a hot day, but I think he was so nervous, with us being favourites and then having the man advantage. He didn't want us to make any silly mistakes. We didn't have that luxury. I remember my shirt was wet through too, although at least I'd been running around! But we couldn't change. To be honest I had been hotter the previous summer when I'd played for England on tour in South America.

We played extremely competently in the second half. Blackburn didn't really threaten us. But we still needed another goal before we could say "that's it." And it came my way. Des Horne crossed from the left towards me. I was running into the area and hammered it first time. I knew it was in as soon as I struck it and when it hit the back of the net it felt tremendous. There was even some controversy about this goal as Blackburn claimed Horne was offside. But what happened was that McGrath was standing on the goal line playing him onside and he jumped off the pitch backwards leaving Des technically offside. But the referee allowed play to continue. Quite rightly in my opinion as I scored!

At least we'd scored a goal ourselves, rather than just win the Cup with an own goal. No one got over-excited. I just got a pat on the back and a couple of handshakes. I think a bit of the shine had been taken off the whole thing for a lot of the lads by Blackburn going down to ten men. And anyway, really we were always of the opinion that it was a team effort. In those days it really was. None of these individualist stars. In fact if anything the real stars were the players who made goals rather than those that finished them off that won the plaudits.

Then I scored again. Des Horne played a short corner routine and crossed it into the box. He mishit it a bit and the ball actually hit the post and came out in front of goal. Woods tried to clear it, but he mishit it too. It fell to me perfectly on the volley. I timed it well and hit it.

I had spent hours in the "dungeon" beneath the stands at Molineux banging balls of the rugged walls and practising shooting on the volley. That paid off then as I turned and hit it cleanly. There was just that small delay while I saw the ball fly into the net and then I knew it was all over. 3-0 versus ten men. We'd won.

I actually should have scored at least twice more in the game, but I got over-excited about the chances and snatched at them whilst not being balanced properly. I was a bit upset about that as no one has scored four goals in a Wembley Cup Final. I was getting so many chances, particularly once Dave had gone off and I should have done better really.

The next thing I knew the whistle went for the end of the game. It was a wonderful feeling. I was last up the steps to pick up my medal. My leg was still sore, although I'd managed to forget about it during the game. We then went on our lap of honour with the Cup and it was tremendous down at our supporters' end.

But when we reached the Blackburn fans' end they reacted very badly. They were throwing stuff. Apple cores, orange peel, money. They threw stuff at us, at the manager and at the referee, who I think they blamed for not sending me off after Dave broke his leg. We walked off and managed to avoid most of this hail of rubbish. The press called it the

"Dustbin Final" because of that. And I think it really was the straw that broke the camel's back when it came to getting the authorities talking about substitutes. They didn't actually come in until some years later (1966), but I think that Cup Final made them discuss it.

When we got down the tunnel I went to their dressing room and asked Ronnie Clayton, who I knew from the England tour I'd been on, how Dave was. There weren't a lot of press men around, but of course we had plenty of coverage in the papers, the Cup Final being the football event of the year.

After a fantastic open top bus tour around the town on the Sunday, later that day I went to have an X-ray on my leg at the Wolverhampton Royal Hospital. Thankfully it was OK. In those days there wasn't much in terms of press aftermath to a big game like that. Not like nowadays when it all gets analysed to hell. I had a few questions about the incident with Dave Whelan, but generally it was accepted that it was an accident. Then we went on a family holiday – a fortnight golfing with my mate Peter Broadbent. He was a good golfer. He used to give me 14 shots and still beat me!

To think that Stan had accused me of throwing the semi-final and now I'd gone and won Wolves the final. He never let you get big-headed though. That was one of his strengths. I remember another occasion when he tried a spot of his 'motivation' on me. It was in 1957 and I'd scored 13 goals in 15 games early in the season, which isn't bad for a winger. Then I'd gone around ten games without finding the back of net. Stan had me into his office and said, "Norman. Sit down. I have had a letter." He read out this letter from a fan which complained about me and the fact that I'd stopped scoring goals. "What do you think of that?" Stan asked. "Who wrote it?" I replied "It's anonymous," says Stan. "He's stupid then," I said. "So why aren't you scoring, Norman?" Stan continued.

And I told him that it was just one of those runs when every shot I struck seemed to hit defenders on the line, or hit the post, or the ball just flew wide and asked Stan what he thought was the reason. He looked at me and, without saying another word, he ripped the letter up.

I then scored in seven of the next eight games! Do you think a fan had written that letter?

JOHN RICHARDS: BORN 9 NOVEMBER 1950, WARRINGTON; 486 GAMES, 194 GOALS

# John Richards

## West Bromwich Albion 3 Wolves 3

## League Division One

## Saturday 28 February 1970

I ONLY EVER had one ambition. All I ever wanted was to play just once for Wolverhampton Wanderers in a first team match. That would have been a fantastic achievement in anyone's life and that was my sole aim every time I walked down the Waterloo Road and into the old entrance at Molineux. From the moment I signed in July 1969 my only goal was to wear the famous gold and black shirt.

MY GAME IS particularly memorable to me, but maybe not to supporters. Obviously it's easy to think about cup finals and titles etcetera, but my first season with Wolves was, for me, a massive sea change to my whole life and it allowed me to fulfil one of my childhood ambitions.

Not many people will know this, but I started as a goalkeeper at the age of eight – the usual reason - no one else wanted to play in that position. It was my junior school side, under 11s, and as I was only eight I was a couple of years younger than most of the other players which meant I had to go in goal. We lost 6-0 and that was the first and last time I played there! I progressed gradually via right-back and right-half and finished up playing inside-right. In the early 1960s we played the old traditional 2-3-5 formation. We did slightly change it when

England won the World Cup. We played more of a 4-3-3, but still with a winger. I always considered myself an inside-forward rather than a centre-forward.

I captained the Warrington town team from when I was 11 and carried on the captaincy role when I moved on to Boteler Grammar School. I was always very quick, my speed was a natural ability, plus I could score goals. That in itself is a gift. I never had any coaching for running at all, or any football skills coaching either. Training was just practice matches or five-a-side. It wasn't as organised as it is now with the youngsters joining Football League club academies.

When I was young professional football was never a consideration, I just enjoyed playing. And not just football. Warrington is a rugby league town, so I also played that sport. I played on the right wing for the town team as an 11-year-old and, as it happened, Steve Kindon played on the left wing. We went our separate ways after that, so it was quite a coincidence that we should end up together at Wolves as a strike force in the 1970s!

I actually didn't see a game of professional football until I was 17 when I went with the Lancashire Schoolboys team to Old Trafford on one of our meet-up weekends. That's followed me through now as I'm not a particularly good watcher of football. As a boy my hero was Jimmy Greaves. He played for Spurs, who won the double in 1961 and he scored tons of goals. I never saw Spurs play apart from on TV, but I admired Greaves' goalscoring. That was my impressionable age and he was the top man.

It was mainly teachers who supported me throughout my progression through county trials in Manchester or Liverpool and into the national Grammar Schoolboys team. There was a teacher called Richard Stobbs who took those of us selected to the trials. Without people like him there was no way I'd have progressed and ended up at Wolves.

AT THE AGE of 18 I did actually play one match for Skelmersdale United, who were trying to put a team together to play in the FA Youth Cup. My friend's dad heard about the trials and took us both along. I got picked and signed to play in their tie against Tranmere Rovers. We lost 3-1 and I scored our goal, the game was played at Prenton Park and someone from Tranmere spoke to me and tried to persuade me to sign, but at that stage I was planning to go to teacher training college.

I really did have every intention of going on to college. I'd got a place sorted out at Chester, dependent on my performance in A levels. But then I was selected to play for England Grammar Schoolboys and that led to me getting the opportunity to play for the Wolves. We played in an Easter tournament in Bognor at the old Butlin's camp. The format was a series of games against other counties and then they selected the national team. It was actually a teacher with the Staffordshire team, Tony Penman, who was also a Wolves scout, that spotted me. By this time I'd made it into the "England probables" side and we played the Arsenal youth team. He approached me after the game and asked if I'd like to have a trial with Wolves.

Within a day of returning home I had Joe Gardiner, Wolves chief scout, knocking on my door. I then had Derby and Sheffield Wednesday scouts coming round, but I'd already given my word to Joe that I'd come down to Molineux for a trial.

The trial turned out to be an actual reserve game at Molineux, the last game of the 1968/69 season. It was against Derby County and we won 4-1. I wasn't intimidated as I'd recently played at Hampden for England in front of a few thousand and there was hardly anyone at this reserve game. I never felt I had lots of pressure on me to make an impression, I just enjoyed myself. I didn't score, but Jimmy Seal scored three and the centre-half Dougie Woodfield got the other. After the game in the dressing room this elderly guy came up to me and said, "Very well played, son. How would you like to play for Wolves?" and I said, "Yes, I would. I'd like that." He went out and I asked Jimmy Seal "Who was that?" and he said, "Oh, that's the chairman, John Ireland." A lovely man who did a great job for the club.

Wolves offered me a one year contract and Chester college agreed to defer my place there for one year. I was in a relatively good position as I had a year to try and make it at Wolves, but had the fall back of my college place if it didn't work out. It was worth the gamble. I was also the eldest in a family of five boys and it probably helped for me to be out earning rather than going to college and being supported for three or four years. I wasn't aware of that then, but in hindsight it must have helped.

THERE WERE DOZENS and dozens of players at Wolves. There must have been about 50 players on the books, plus 15 or 16 apprentices. I changed in the away team dressing room then as the home dressing room was reserved for the first team squad. We were all cramped together. I started in the West Midland League team, which was basically the third team. I did quite well and got into the reserves within a matter of weeks. It was quite a quick step up, but making that next step up to the first team seemed such a long way away.

Because I'd come into the game late it took me a while to get up to speed from a fitness point of view. The pre-season training just killed me. We went cross-country running at Cannock Chase. Up and down the hills and then we'd do weights. I'd never done that before and it really took its toll. I got weaker before I got stronger. It was difficult to make an impression to start off with. Then I got stronger and I progressed up to the reserves quickly and started scoring goals. The game which really made an impression and made people sit up and take notice was when we won 5-2 at Blackburn and I scored all five. They probably thought, "Who's this Richards guy?"

There was so much happening within the club around then. It was a very memorable season. The first team had won the first four or five matches in a cracking start to the season, and then there was the situation with Peter Knowles. He decided to pack in football just before his 24th birthday and follow his faith as a Jehovah's Witness, as he didn't think football and his beliefs were compatible. The club thought he would be back. They didn't think he'd stick to his guns and they retained his registration for years afterwards. To replace him they bought Mike O'Grady from Leeds, a good winger. So it was quite an exciting and interesting time. There was a lot of publicity about us as we were doing well. I wanted to be part of that. I was sad that I didn't get to play with Peter Knowles, though, as I thought he was a great player. He was only five or so years older than me and we could have had several years playing together.

I WAS STILL scoring the goals in the reserves and that elevated me to being included in the first team squad for the occasional away game, when they'd take 13 or 14 players with them, and I helped Sammy Chung put out the kit and boots. It was great travelling as a non-playing reserve as you got a taste of what it was like in the changing room before a big match. Some of the other reserve teamers had been getting that. When it happened the first time however, the circumstances surrounding it were rather different.

I shared lodgings with a lad called Barry Powell, who was an apprentice then, at a house by Bantock Park. We shared a room together. Our landlady was Mrs Eagle. On the Saturday before Christmas I woke up in the morning expecting to play for the reserves and there was someone throwing a stone at the window from outside. Barry got up and looked out and he said, "It's Sammy!" It was Sammy Chung, the first team coach. The first team bus was outside and apparently Hughie Curran had been taken sick overnight so they needed a forward to make up the squad. I quickly changed and went along with them to Nottingham Forest. Of course there was only one sub in those days and I was making up a party of 14, so I didn't really expect to play. However, it was great experience because, at that stage, I was still in awe of the first teamers. I was still calling them "Mr Bailey", and so on. That was my first taste of the action, and I loved it. I'm glad that wasn't my debut as I wouldn't have had time to tell anyone, but it was exciting.

Then I was back in the reserves for a while before Derek Dougan got a record suspension for getting sent off, which put him out for seven or eight weeks and McGarry was forced to try different combinations up front alongside Hughie Curran to see what would work. He tried Frank Munro, Jimmy McCalliog and Derek Clarke, one of the famous Clarke brothers who all played league football.

They had all performed OK and then one week, on the Thursday, I was asked to go alongside Hughie when the first team were rehearsing free kicks and set pieces. Previously I'd played for the reserve team attack against the first team defence. Now I was in the first team attack playing against the reserves' defence. I thought I might be in with a chance and, on the Friday, Bill McGarry called me in and told me, "You're going to be playing against West Brom tomorrow." McGarry had quite a reputation for the way that he dealt with young players and how he introduced them slowly into the first team, and here I was being thrown straight into the deep end at the Hawthorns!

However, I do think he and Sammy knew I was very naïve and even ignorant at the time. I'd never really been anywhere, I wasn't aware of the significance of the intense rivalry with West Brom and so I couldn't have been intimidated by it. In some ways I was the ideal candidate to play. And when Bill told me I was elated. I didn't think, "Oh, no. Not West Brom." I thought "fantastic!" The first thing I did was to let my parents know, I wasn't sure they would be able to come to the game because they didn't have a car. Fortunately, my mum managed to arrange a lift with an old school pal of mine, Chris Miller. I was delighted she could get to the game because she had always supported me, in fact all of us. It was her more than anyone who encouraged me. That night I thought about how I'd managed to achieve my ambition. It might not be Molineux, but I was going to be playing in the Wolves first team. I would be achieving my goal. I think when you're young and late into the game you just go with things and don't let them overawe you. I never had any worries in my mind that I wasn't going to play well, that the Albion defence would make a fool of me or intimidate me.

THE DAY OF the match came and I was so excited. I woke up early and got ready to go. But the thing is we didn't have to report until half past twelve as it's only 25 minutes to West Brom, I was kicking my heels all morning. I just wanted to get on with it. Get there and play. But this Saturday morning dragged on for ever. That was the worst bit.

On the coach Sammy came up and said the Boss wanted to have a word with me. So I went down to the front of the bus where McGarry sat and he was great. He said, "You know you're playing up front with Hughie. Just work hard. If you lose the ball, get behind it and defend from the front." That was always his philosophy. It was as simple as that. It wasn't a big speech or anything; just, "Go out and do what you've done with the reserves."

The best bit of all was that when we got to the ground I saw my mother, she was there by the players' entrance when we got off the coach. That really made my day.

Then in the changing room it felt just like a reserve game – apart from the fact I was changing, for the first time, alongside Jim McCalliog, Mike Bailey, Frank Munro, Bernard Shaw and Hughie Curran. Like any other person making your debut, they all talked to me, saying all the right things. But it just went straight through me. I knew I could fit in, though, as the reserves played exactly the same way as the first team, so I knew what was expected. I can't recall Hughie saying anything particular other than to wish me good luck. He knew that I'd be alright because McGarry had picked me. Simple as that.

The only thing that really hit me was when we ran out. That was the only bit that made me realise that this wasn't like any other game; that this was far more than anything I'd experienced previously. There was no on-pitch warm up in those days. We warmed up in the dressing room, so I hadn't been out on to the pitch. Also, we didn't go out two teams together. We went out first, and the noise when we came out of the tunnel - it made me hesitate and realise that I'd never been in that sort of environment before. It took your breath away. I also tried to spot my mum in the crowd, I was that naïve! I'd always been able to whenever I'd played before. But there was no way I was able to do that with the ground so full.

The game itself felt good. I thought I did alright. It wasn't brilliant for me or the team, but it was good enough. We played well to start with and went ahead thanks to an early Hughie Curran penalty after McCalliog was fouled by Fraser. Albion were due at Wembley the following week for the League Cup Final, but it didn't mean that they were any the less competitive, local pride was at stake!

They equalised shortly afterwards, but then we went back in front with a Mike O'Grady goal. I can still remember it vividly. He hit this ball from outside the box and it whistled past my head and screamed into the top corner. It was a fantastic goal.

Hughie got another and someone scored for West Brom, I can't remember who. You tend to blank opposition goals from your mind. Hughie's second was the most phenomenal header. This ball came across from the right and he headed it so hard. It flew into the net. I thought, "God, how do you head the ball so hard?" There was only five minutes to go and we were leading 3-2 and hanging on for our lives. I was chasing about a lot, the exuberance of youth. A couple of minutes to go and they scrambled this goal and I felt horrible. It was an awful feeling that they should have equalised at the death like that. There was the elation of playing in the match and then the disappointment of conceding late on. In the dressing room afterwards everyone felt so low. Not a lot was said, but everyone was disappointed. I think it was normal then for there to be little discussion as we always had a cooling-off period to avoid things being said in the heat of the moment. I think that was wise.

THAT DAY THE captain, Mike Bailey, made the most impression on me. He spoke to me, telling me where to make runs and when to conserve my energy, to stop chasing lost causes. He made the game easy for me. It wasn't really until after he left the club some years later that I truly realised the influence he had. He was very commanding and calm in the tradition of great Wolves captains from Cullis through Wright and Slater to Flowers; revered half-backs who led their men from midfield. Mike's loss was a massive one for the club when he eventually went and I don't think he's ever truly been replaced to this day.

Hughie Curran also impressed me. He was an unsung hero at Wolves, because Derek Dougan was such a character. Hughie was the best header of the ball that I ever played with. He was a good player and unappreciated for his talents really. I suppose Waggy (Dave Wagstaffe) and Dougan were the stars as such. When I forged my partnership with Dougan that brought so many goals in the early 70s, we complemented each other perfectly. His job was to win the ball in the air and mine was to get past him and on to the flick-ons. Doog was superb in the air and we were devastating for two-and-a-half years. A lot of the credit for the success of our partnership has to go to players such as Dave Wagstaffe and Kenny Hibbitt who supplied all the crosses. Also, to the manager. Initially, McGarry had us playing down the channels which suited our natural feet, me on the right and Dougan on the left. But Bill switched us so that I was making cross-over runs from the left to the right and on to my naturally stronger foot; the same applied to Doog. It worked brilliantly. It confused defenders who were always crossing over to try to keep with us and created mayhem for us to take advantage of.

Funnily enough Dougan was an easy character to get on with, despite him being the elder statesman of the team. He was the PFA rep and I took over from him so we had some common ground. When Hughie Curran was sold to Oxford it became me or Bobby Gould for the slot alongside Dougan and eventually I claimed it, through weight of goals as much as anything else.

It all culminated in the League Cup win in 1974, but we'd come so close previously in two FA Cup semi-finals and a UEFA Cup Final. We should have won more really. That successful Wolves side began to break up as the older group of Wagstaffe, Bailey, Dougan, Munro and, to a certain extent, Phil Parkes came to the end. McGarry tried to replace them like for like, but the players that came in, while good, did not really fit and we ended up being relegated in 1976. The newcomers didn't suit the style we'd been playing and that all ended up with Bill McGarry getting the sack when we went down.

ONE OF THE best bits of my debut day came as I got back on the bus. I can always remember meeting my mum there. She was so excited. They had to rush off to get home as it was a long way to Warrington, but it was fantastic to see her. It topped off a great day.

When we got back to Molineux I did what I always did after reserve team games and went into the social club with some of the players for our usual shandy before heading back to the digs. Only this time I had an ulterior motive. I was waiting for the *Saturday Pink* to arrive. They always dropped off a couple of dozen about half past six. I couldn't wait to get a copy and read what Phil Morgan, the Wolves' reporter, had to say about my debut. The report didn't mention me too much apart from me making my first start and calling me a workaholic for all the running I did, but I think that's mainly because in those days there wasn't the technology of today when things can be sent down the line at a moment's notice. Then they had to typeset the whole thing so really it was just a report of the main action and goals. Goalscorers' names were always in bold, I remember.

Then I just went back to my digs and stayed in. No big celebrations for me. After all I may have fulfilled my ambition, but it wasn't as if I'd lit up the team or we'd won. I couldn't stop playing the game over in my head; the things I'd done well and not done so well. My main concern then was looking forward. Had I done well enough to keep my place in the team?

The short answer to that was "no", although I did play in the following three games, I was dropped when Dougan came back. But then I knew I was only filling in for him anyway.

When I think back on that time I realise that Bill McGarry didn't really gee you up for playing, even an inexperienced youngster. He was quite fearsome and was quick to dish out the odd kick up the backside to anyone who he thought wasn't pulling their weight. The good cop to McGarry's bad cop was Sammy Chung, he was a great coach, the best I have ever worked with. He would take the young lads to one side. He took us on a Thursday afternoon for extra training. All the 18-20 year olds in the first and reserve teams. The likes of me, Kenny Hibbitt, Bertie Lutton and Paul Walker. Sammy was excellent at his job and made a good team with McGarry, he put his arm around you and encouraged while the manager doled out the bollockings!

JUST AS AN aside, at the end of my debut season, when I knew I was going to be staying at Wolves, the youth team went on a tour of Africa, Malawi and Zambia, and I went as an over age player. It was an incredible experience. It was the first time I'd been on a plane, or been abroad. We saw abject poverty in both countries, some of us were billeted in the community with families in the copper mining districts. As we were a youth team we played against the national school team in Zambia, but a lot of the opposing players were adults still at school, so actually we were often playing men. The tour went well for me as I scored a lot of goals. We won the three 'internationals' in Zambia, but drew with the Malawi under-21 team. That was a very fierce game, probably the most ferocious I ever played in. A couple of the Malawi team started kicking and some of our lads retaliated. Remember we were all young. It ended up a near riot and we had to be locked in our dressing room at the end of the game for over an hour for our own safety. That was quite an experience.

But at the end of that tour I learned that I had done enough to earn a new, three year contract. I decided to forget about teaching and concentrate on playing for Wolves and, thankfully, it paid off. I did keep on with my education though as we had a lot of spare time and I wanted to make use of it. I went to Wulfrun College and did a cost and works accountancy course which stood me in good stead.

I spent the next season developing in the reserves after McGarry brought in Bobby Gould in the summer. But that season did me the power of good. I built my confidence and impressed McGarry enough to stay around the fringes of the first team, before really making the breakthrough in 1972. I also learnt about some of the realities of football the hard way. I remember going to McGarry and telling him that I was fed up with being on the bench. I wanted to play. That was it then. I was out of the first team squad for about two months. McGarry taught me a lesson! It was an expensive one because I lost out on first team squad bonus money.

I soon learned to do things a different way, I decided to keep my head down and work. Eventually my chance came and then it was up to me to take it.

In November 1971 I was given the chance to start against Derby. We won 2-1 at Molineux and I scored both goals. That was the kick-start for me and I felt I was a first teamer then. It's funny how things happened for me around my birthday in November. That Blackburn game when I'd scored five in the reserves was also in November. It was definitely my lucky month.

MIKE BAILEY: BORN 27 FEBRUARY 1942, WISBECH; 436 GAMES, 25 GOALS

# Mike Bailey

## Wolves 2 Manchester City 1

## League Cup Final

## Saturday 2 March 1974

I REMEMBER THE moment. It was when John Richards scored to put us one up against Liverpool in the League Cup quarter-final. It was that moment that I remember talking to Jimmy McCalliog (who won the FA Cup with Sheffield Wednesday), saying he felt their name was on the cup from the early rounds and I had that feeling.

Lifting a trophy at Wembley as a captain is the most special thing in football, so that victory gave me the opportunity to do it; to fulfil my dreams. I was very fortunate in that sense. So I have to choose the 1974 League Cup win as my most memorable game.

If you're talking pure football, however, then the best we ever played (in my view) when I was at Wolves was in the EUFA Cup against Porto, the Portuguese giants, the season after we won the League Cup. We were 4-1 down after the first leg to Porto and actually had been 3-0 down and I scored to get us back in the game and grab a crucial away goal. Then we got them back to Molineeux and it was the best game I'd ever seen us play. We were buzzing on the night. The surface was wet on top. It was firm, but zippy. You just had to stroke the ball to pass it effortlessly.

We hit the bar and post in the first 15 minutes and in between those near misses I prodded in a John Richards shot to give us some hope. We scored two more goals, Steve Daly nodded in and the Doog scored with another header. We went in at half time 3-0 up and were in the next round with 45 minutes to play due to my away goal in Portugal which counted double if scores were equal after two legs.

After half-time we kept the tempo up. I thought we were playing so well we'd get another goal but for all our efforts we failed to score again. I still don't quite believe it. On the night we were great. We were playing one touch football , two touch football and carved them apart. With a few minutes to go they won a corner which they played in low and to the near post. Somehow the ball finished up in the back of our net!! Porto had achieved the all important away goal and we lost the tie. But it cannot compare with winning at Wembley.

I STARTED MY professional career at Charlton at 17 years-old. I made my first team debut at 18 and became captain. I won five England under-23 caps and a couple of full caps and might have had a chance of being in the 1966 World Cup squad, but for a badly broken leg in the season leading up to the tournament.

When I was 23-years-old the Charlton manager, Bob Stokoe, called me in and said, "Wolves want to talk to you. Would you like to go up there?" I said "yes" as it was such a shock that Charlton were prepared to leg me go. Both clubs were in the Second Division at the time, but obviously Wolves were a huge name when I was growing up. It's funny how it works, but on one of the England under-23 trips I shared a room with Ernie Hunt, who was at Swindon at the time, and we got on so well, we just talked through the night. I couldn't believe how well we got on, or that we had a game the next day, as we just talked and talked and talked. Ernie and I both had decent games and we won. He was then transferred to Wolves and when Charlton played at Wolves in the League that season I went into the Wolves dressing-room to see him. The Wolves manager, Ronnie Allen, said to me, "Oh, we could do with you here. We are getting a good side together" So the thought had been there for a while.

I came up to Wolverhampton and saw Ronnie Allen and the Chairman John Ireland. They sold me the club and asked me if I wanted to sign. I asked for time to think it over and talk to my wife Barbara as it obviously meant uprooting and moving to the Midlands. But John Ireland said, "No, we need it sorting out today" So I phoned Barbara and we agreed it was right. I felt I had a better chance of winning things and playing, hopefully, in the First Division. So I signed.

When I came back to tidy things up at Charlton, Bob Stokoe was surprised I'd signed so quickly. He thought I might hang on and wait to see if there would be any interest from other clubs now it was known that Charlton were prepared to sell me. In fact I later heard that Spurs were interested, but I didn't know at the time. John Ireland knew what he was doing when he made me sign there and then as he sensed that I might waver if I went back home.

In fact, if I'd known Spurs had been interested I probably would not have signed as quickly as I did, Spurs were my father's favourite team and one I naturally followed as a lad because of him.

In fact I think I was really fortunate that John Ireland persuaded me so forcefully to come as I had 11 wonderful years at Wolves and I would not have missed it for the world. We had a fantastic life and loved the Midlands and have made really good friends who we still continue to see.

Ronnie Allen had a great eye for a player. He brought in Derek Parkin, Frank Munro, Dave Wagstaffe, Peter Knowles, Kenny Hibbitt, Derek Dougan and myself. They were all very talented players who served the club well for a number of years. Plus we were good enough players not to need too much coaching. All we did was play five-a-side every day and if there was a problem on the field we were capable of sorting it out ourselves. He invested in quality. His style was very relaxed. He didn't lecture, he just talked about football saying, "Come on, keep your passing going", or "See if you can get a few more crosses in". That sort of thing.

Because things were so relaxed we enjoyed ourselves and our football. I always remember that we used to play cricket in the dressing room as a warm up. We had a big dressing room and we played with a bat and the batsman had to play defensively and give catches and everyone else was around trying to take them. That as a warm up worked well for sharpening us up mentally as much as anything.

And the other basis of why we were so successful was that the players all went round together. It just sort of happened, rather than being a conscious thing. We all got on well. We were mostly around the same age. We'd go out on a Saturday after the game , with our wives. We were very much together on the pitch and off it socially and that continues to this day, especially through the former players' association.

People often ask what my strengths were. I was a ball winner, but I also had a good range of passes. My stock ball probably was right to left. I didn't even have to look where Waggy was out there on the wing. I received the ball and bang, I found him. I probably left Hibby out in the cold on the right because I was always looking for Waggy. I could have let the ball run across me and fired it out to the other wing, but I just had this telepathic relationship with Waggy.

I was captain of the side and I simply wanted to win every game. I'd psyche the palyers up before the match and make sure that we were performing to our best. I enjoyed competing. The bigger the game the better and I really did want to win. I remember once at Portsmouth we were 2-0 down and I went into three tackles in quick seccession just in front of the directors' box. I won the first and it broke loose and I went through the next one and won it and then it broke loose again aand I won the third. That was just before half-time and it seemed to lift everyone. We got back into the game and early into the second half I made a forward run and beat the offside trap and went right through and beat the keeper to score That lifted everyone again and we ended up winning 3-2 and gave me a lot of satisfaction. The chaiman met us off the train at low level station and shook every player's hand he was so pleased.

I could be quite terse, I did use to give the lads some leather at times and Steve Daly once went up to my wife and said, "How do you live with him? Is he like that at home?" But I just wanted to win and if I could see that someone wasn't doing as much as he could I'd go over and have a quiet word. But equally if someone did well I would be the first to praise too.

Then Bill McGarry came in and took us on a stage and we began to make it into semi-finals and finishing in the top six. We'd been disappointed by the change as we'd all liked Ronnie and he'd bought most of us, but you have to accept that kind of thing and get on with it. Bill brought a bit more discipline and he did more physical work in training, making us run up the terraces to the back of the stands. Under him tactically we became more solid. Where previously we'd perhaps been simply all out attack and we'd try to score more goals than them and quite often draw wwhen we should have won and maybe lose when we should have drawn, Bill's background as a half-back made us harder to beat and that got us more consistent results. In fact when we got to the FA Cup semi-final in 1972/73 we only conceded one goal in the whole competition, but that was the goal that Leeds scored to put us out.

I remember that day Frank Munro and I weren't playing as we had both been injured. Bill didn't feel that he could gamble on us for such an important match. I eventually went on as a substitute and hit the bar. Then within minutes, Leeds, being the side they were grinding out results under Revie, scored when the ball bobbed around in our area and we didn't get it away. They put it into our net and we were out.

THE PREVIOUS SEASON we also reached the UEFA Cup Final. On the way there we beat Coimbra of Portugal, Den Haag (when the Dutch right-back scored three own goals in the two legs. I actually felt very sorry for him), Carl Zeiss Jena and then Juventus. We beat them 2-0 at Molineux. They were such a huge name and they had Helmut Haller, their star, who'd played and scored for West Germany in the 1966 World Cup Final. I was injured for the return in Turin. For that, McGarry came up with a brilliant piece of thinking. He brought John Charles in as an interpreter. I'd always admired him. He was my favourite player and was a legend over there, having played for the club with such distinction. I remember we were getting out of the coach at the ground and Big John got off first and the crowd went wild. The man who'd looked after John's boots came over and kissed his feet in the dressing rooms before the game.

The reaction in the stadium was just incredible. I went out to sit on the bench to watch the game and walked out of the tunnel entrance to John Charles. As we emerged the whole stadium stood up and shouted, "Charlo, Charlo, Charlo!" In effect they were chanting against their own side as he was with us. It was such a psychological blow and I think it inspired us to a goalless draw. Juventus hadn't been beaten at home in Europe for years, so it was one hell of a result.

Then, of course, we ended up playing Spurs in the final which was such a flat balloon. It just felt like any other league game. It's supposed to be special playing in a top European Final, but it really was just like any normal First Division game. I am sure we'd have won it had it been a foreign team. But as it was all the players knew each other and Martin Chivers hit two bulletts in the first leg at Molineux, to score two vital goals and win the Cup for Spurs. We could not make up the deficit at White Hart Lane and Spurs won the cup. To lose over two legs was a great disappointment to us.

THE LEAGUE CUP recently has been seen as a bit of a Mickey Mouse cup. But back in the 1970s it had a bit of recognition. Teams had really started putting out their main sides and were attracting big crowds. It had become a money spinner and then there was the European place for the winners.

I remember beating Halifax comfortably in round two, then Tranmere after a replay and hammering Exeter. Then we got to the tough games. In the quarter-final we drew Liverpool, but significantly it was at home. John Richards scored in typically predatory fashion to see them off 1-0 which shows how McGarry's more defensive philosophy paid off. We'd thought that because we'd drawn them at home we had a good chance and we were really geared up for it. We played really solidly and didn't give them anything away and we were patient. Then John put in the winner for us.

The funny thing about that game was that it was played on a Wednesday afternoon as we had to play in daylight hours because of the national energy crisis which was biting heavily in Britain at the time.we weren't allowed to use the floodlights so had to play during the afternoon. There was also the three-day working week which seemingly everyone else was on except us footballers!

Our strike partnership of Dougan and Richards thrived on the two wingers that supplied Derek with a great service. But we could also play things through in the channels and Doog's pace and also John's could get them in. John was also so strong on the turn in the box and he always got his shots off quickly. He was one of those strikers who didn't have to hit the ball cleanly to get it into the net. He could score all sorts of types of goals: off his knees, headers,flicks and powerful shots. He was simply an out and out goalscorer. So we had this variety of options which made us a top side and worked really well. John in fact scored in every round of that competition except against Tranmere in the two third round games.

Norwich in the semis was a tough tie. They actually got relegated that season, but we were happy to have the away leg first. It's how we would have planned it before the draw. We just wanted to draw at Carrow Road and we managed it thanks to another John Richards goal. Norwich battled, though, as this was their realease from the pressure of the relegation scrap.

Then we won the home leg with a simple classic Wolves goal. Phil Parkes launched the ball forwards, Doog flicked it on and John used his pace and finishing ability to slot the decisive goal. We'd made it through to Wembley.

That gave us credibility that this team had come back from having been relegaated in the mid-60s and here we are now at Wembley in a cup final. We actually felt it was the beginning of a new successful era for the club.

All the usual stuff was happening for a Cup Final: songs, suits, superstitions, all the rest of it. I remember the song. We had to call our names out. "I'm Mike Bailey. I'm a midfielder" All that kind of thing. We were also getting interviews and the press were having to pay for an interview which they were quite happy to do. That all went into a pool for the players to share. Derek Dougan was in charge of that as he was the PFA rep. It all helped bring the team together. Even though the press tended to want Derek, myself and Waggy, so we had more work to do, we felt it was fair that we shared everything out. So that's what we did.

I actually suggested to Bill McGarry to turn our strip around and have black shirts and gold shorts and have the badge in gold for the final as I thought it would look fantastic for this special occasion, but the referee was always in black in those days so we couldn't. Nowadays of course they wear all sorts of colours so it would have been allowed. However the track suits we left the dressing room in were black top and gold bottoms and they looked great.

We did have a few injuries leading up to the final. Phil Parkes, who was our normal goalkeeper, was out and so Gary Pierce, his understudy played. Then John Richards and I were injured and were struggling to make the team. I had a hamstring and John had a torn stomach muscle. We didn't play for three weeks beforehand and we were worried we'd miss the game. We were only doing light training and the other lads were ribbing us saying, "Oh, thats right. You have a little jog and then we'll see you on Saturday at Wembley!" We really got some stick. The gaffer also said we couldn't be tackled in the five-a-sides which led to more mickey-taking. Thankfully we both made it. That, of course, gave McGarry selection problems as the lads who had been playing for the previous three weeks had done well. He ended up having to choose between Kenny Hibbit and Barry Powell for the last midfield spot alongside me. He went with Kenny in the end. Sunderland played on the right of me, Kenny to the left. Two of the most talented players I have played with. I thought they were just great. I was just happy to be playing.

I'd played at Wembley once for England so it was not completely strange. The pitch was unbelievable, although the Horse of the Year Show in 1970 had meant the original famous pitch which gave everyone cramp had to be taken up. This one wasn't so demanding, although you still always heard of players suffering.

We went away to the sleepy seaside resort of Worthing in Sussex a week beforehand. Most of the residents in the hotel were elderly but they seemed to enjoy us being there. The lads made a bit of fuss of them and I actually thought they were disappointed when we moved out on Friday to a hotel nearer to Wembley. As the coach left they waved us off wishing us good luck, I am quite sure they watched us on the box and would have cheered us on.

I slept really well the night before the final. After breakfast I had a walk in the extensive grounds of the hotel, was very relaxed, some of the lads did the same, others read the papers, they seemed a very calm and focused bunch of lads enjoying every moment. It was if they did not want to miss anything. Eventually we boarded the coach dressed in our club suits and made our way to Wembley. On reaching Wembley Way it was an awesome sight. The day was sunny and bright and all we could see was old gold and black. Our fans surrounded our coach and I swear they carried us, coach and all on their shoulders the last mile to the magnificent Wembley Stadium.

Once in the dressing room we then made our way to the pitch to soak up the early atmosphere and of course met our opponents for the first time. We were actually concerned as one would be of the very talented forward line of the opposition: Marsh, Law, Lee, Summerbee, goals could come from anywhere and Bell was another potential danger.

Back in the dressing room McGarry gave words of encouragement: "We've got this far – let's go on and win it." As I got changed I felt we had done the hard work getting this far and this was the huge bonus. The bell sounded and we gathered in the tunnel and walked out onto the pitch to an unbelievable atmosphere. The next thing I knew I'd been introduced to the Duke of Kent and traditionally I introduced him to the rest of the team. After the anthem , which was very emotional we took our positions to kick off. We started off very brightly much sharper, more determined than City – closed them down, won more tackles and had some early confidence-boosters with slick moves which caused them problems. They eventually came back at us and it evened itself out until we worked a ball out to the right to Alan Sunderland who skipped past a full-back, laid the ball back to Geoff Palmer, whose cross found Kenny Hibbit on the edge of the box and he volleyed it into the net with one minute to go before half time. What a time to score!!

Now Gary Pierce had not played many games in the first team. It was actually his 23rd birthday and it was certainly one to remember for the rest of his life. He really was inspired. Wembley can do that to people sometimes and sometimes it can make them curl up and die, but Gary was magnificent that day. It must rank as the best game he played in his life. But for me - apart from Gary - the real success of the day was the two centre-backs. Frank Munro and John Mcalle were absolutely outstanding. They baarely gave their two front lads - Franny Lee and Denis Law a kick. John McAlle won plenty of tackles that he just didn't deserve to win. That's when it comes down to who wants it the most. He would simply come out with the ball and pass it nice and simple to the nearest Gold shirt. Job done. They were well supported by full-backs Geoff Palmer and Derek Parkin. Derek had a real ding-dong with city's captain Mike Summerbee and came out on top of that battle. When we came out for the second half that was the time when Gary came into his own because they put us under tremendous pressure. He came out and leapt for crosses. His handling was superb, he never spilled anything and he went down at people's feet a couple of times when they got through and as he kept making these saves, confidence spread throughout the team.

But then they equalised. What happened was they came down the left and Marshy had it. I was tracking him. He went to go down the line and then all of a sudden he pulled it back on to his favoured foot. After the game McGarry said I wasn't close enough to him. In actual fact I could have blocked it, but my standing foot went and that was enough for Rodney to cross the ball in. It caught us out at the back post and Colin Bell ran in and scored.

They then had us on the rack. We were really under the cosh. They hit the bar, missed a couple of sitters and we hacked a couple off the line. Gary was great and Frank and John were getting their bodies in the way of any goal bound shots.

It was then I felt I really had to get hold of the game. We kept giving the ball away. You cannot do that at Wembley because you don't get it back as the pitch is so wide. We kept knocking long balls down the line, but they were going straight to Man City and allowing them to put us under more pressure. I started demanding the ball more from the back and played a few more short passes bringing more players into the game and gradually worked our way back and kept more possession to relieve the pressure.

It was about this time John Richards started feeling his stomach injury, but McGarry couldn't take him off because Dave Wagstaffe was also suffering with a hamstring injury and in the end he had to come off - this was a big blow as Waggy's ability to go past defenders and supply the crosses for big Doog was second to none. Barry Powell replaced Waggy and fitted in brilliantly for one so young. John stayed on and fortunately for us was there to score the winning goal.

With ten minutes to go I got the ball from Alan Sunderland and from the corner of my eye I saw Sundy move forward into the channels and I whipped the ball into him, it was just enough to tempt the defender into the tackle and Sundy pulled his foot away to let it run across him. He saw John and crossed it low, fortunately it took a deflection off Rodney Marsh and fell into John Richards' path. It was that bit of luck that wins cups and John made the most of it by shooting into the corner of Man City's net to put us 2-1 up with minutes to play.

We only realised the significance of that goal for John when his injury got the better of him straight after the game and he didn't play again that season. He went on to become a regular top scorer for the club though, and no Wolves fan will ever forget the sight of that ball nestling in the bottom corner of the net. It certainly made me leap for joy!

Then I really knew we were going to win it. Just as I had felt it against Liverpool. It's just how things go your way. We'd scored against Liverpool and we'd been drawn away from home in the semi-final first leg. Now we were leading again in the final. It all seemed to fit a pattern - our name was definitely on that cup.

I just couldn't believe we had won. Especially having City put us under so much pressure in the second half and us coming back from an equaliser. We played out the last few minutes without too many scares and then the full-time whistle blew. It was just such a relief having achieved winning a major trophy for the club. Somewhere along the line we felt we now belonged in some small way to creating our own bit of Wolves history along with the great teams of the past.

The Man City lads were brilliant. At the League Cup Final the losers go up first and although they must have been feeling sick they were really sportsmanlike and applauded us up the stairs. The only exception was Rodney Marsh and it wasn't because he was unsporting at all, but he was so distraught that it was his deflection that had let in John to score the winner.

For us it was really really memorable and was everything that you hope a Wembley Cup Final can be. Just to walk up those steps where the Billy Wrights and the Bobby Moores haave walked - it was magnificent. You are fulfilling a schoolboy ambition. Those moments you have played out in your backyard at home time and time again.

All the gold and black was a blur when we took the cup to where our supporters were and those were fantstic moments. All the better becaause people who'd had long careers like Doog and Bil McGarry had never actually won anything before - so it was very special indeed.

Then we had a function in the evening at the London Hilton. I kept the Cup and took it to bed with me. Next thing I knew there was a panic because no one else knew where it was. The manager and directors thought the cup had been lost, but I had it in bed all night. Steven Gerrard did that when Liverpool won the European Cup in 2005, but I'd done it over 30 years previously!!

We then went back to Wolverhampton Town Hall and showed the cup in the main square, which was full of our wonderful supporters , but then we had to go back to london again because it was the PFA Footballer of the Year Awards. So it really was a magical magical weekend.

I even had the cup for a couple of days after that. I also let my son Andrew take the cup into his school. He was only six at the time and it was a proud moment for him I then had to give it back on the Tuesday - I think the insurers were worried about ever seeing it again!!

It was a huge thing for the town because it meant their pride was back. Wolves were back where they belonged. We were enormously proud to play for this great club and felt that this could be the beginnings of big things again. Not least because it also meant automatic qualifications for the UEFA Cup the following season.

I would have liked to have pushed on from there because I was coming towards the end of my career, but it turned out that winning the League Cup was the pinnacle rather than the start of something. Partly because we'd come so close in other cups - the FA Cup twice and the UEFA Cup. But at least we had something to say "I was part of that".

DEREK PARKIN: BORN 2 JANUARY 1948, NEWCASTLE-UPON-TYNE; 609 GAMES, 6 GOALS

# Derek Parkin

## Wolves 1 Nottingham Forest 1
## League Cup Final
## Saturday 15 March 1980

THE WEEK I was transferred to the Wolves in February 1968, on the Monday I passed my driving test, on Tuesday I bought a car to celebrate, on the Wednesday we found out my wife was pregnant and then on the Thursday, St Valentine's day, I signed. It doesn't get much better than that!

I was delighted because I wanted to play First Division football. I'd started at Huddersfield, because a scout called Harry Hooper, whose son was actually a former Wolves player, spotted me playing for Northumberland Boys. I had a few trials before being asked to sign as an apprentice under manager Tom Johnston. I was lucky enough to play in the first team at 16 because of injuries and became a regular around my 18th birthday.

Of course at Huddersfield the left-back was World Cup winner Ray Wilson. I picked up things from him. He was superb, slimly built and like lightning, so quick. I didn't actively learn from him by pestering him for tips or anything, but if you don't pick up hints and tips from someone like that you really shouldn't be playing.

When the Wolves signed me they paid a record fee for a full-back, I'd played a few games by then and really enjoyed the pressure of a matchday and the buzz of the crowd. I've never lost that, so there wasn't any pressure from being a record buy. If I said I was never nervous I'd be lying, but once the whistle went I'd be off.

But what I didn't know was that when I got back to Huddersfield to collect my boots having signed, there were about five or six clubs waiting to sign me. I remember Tottenham was one of them and Nottingham Forest was another. So things could have been very different! But I was excited to be in the First Division and playing in that great team and finding your name in the paper. Then seeing yourself on TV for the first time, you can't get your breath. It just felt so strange – but so good.

The players in that Wolves side were the likes of Derek Dougan, Mike Bailey and Dave Wagstaffe. I'd actually played well against them over Easter 1967, the season Wolves eventually won promotion back to Division One. On the back of that Ronnie Allen signed me the following year. He was a good manager, Ronnie. Bill McGarry inherited a lot of good players that he'd bought and had success with them, so Ronnie never really gets the credit he deserves. He liked people who played, whereas McGarry was a disciplinarian. Ronnie was a bit more flexible, but that was possibly his downfall. Sometimes players need a rollicking and that's what McGarry did. He went straight in for people and it worked for him.

Ronnie's record in the transfer market was remarkable – me, Doog, Mike Bailey; then Kenny Hibbitt was the best five grand ever spent. Look what he did for Wolves.

I WAS ACTUALLY always a right-back. It was only when I came to Wolves and Bill McGarry took over that I swapped sides. There was no natural left-back at the club at the time as Bobby Thompson had moved to Birmingham and Bill asked me to switch over. It worried me at first as I was right-footed and I did find it a problem for a while. I wasn't really left footed at all. I was OK, and I gave it a go, because it meant I was in the team. It was a problem, though, as every time I came forward I had to come inside on to my right foot. I did try to improve, but everyone's got their restrictions. Mind you I was always in the team and he didn't bother to buy a replacement left-footed player, so I must have done OK.

I always thought of myself as a steady full-back and I used to bide my time before tackling. Tackling is all about timing, choosing your moment to win the ball. Not brute force. Anyway I wasn't an overtly physical kind of player. My nickname was "Squeak" because of my high voice. Mike Bailey always claimed it was him that came up with it. But then so does the Doog. Mike was a great skipper and I think it might actually have been him as he was the right half in front of me. So as I ran past him on an overlapping run I used to shout for the ball. And I was so young that my voice hadn't broke properly and throughout the game my voice got higher and higher, and it just stuck. Doog still calls it me even now. He's a real character, the Doog. I know he's had his critics, but I speak as I find and as far as I'm concerned he's a good fellow and I'm not going to be swayed by anyone else. He's always been good to me.

Bill McGarry did admit that he had probably spoilt my chances of going further international wise by playing me on the left hand side, because early on I played for the under-23s and for the Football League, but I never got that full England call up. Alf Ramsey actually took the under-23s for training and he was a very good manager, very professional

I played for the Football League for the Scottish League at Hampden and I played with basically the whole 1966 World Cup team. I always used to sweat profusely when I played, mainly because of all the running I was doing and all the effort I put in, but that day I was alongside Bobby Moore and it was the easiest game I have ever played. Every time I got into trouble Bobby was there to receive a pass off me. It was so simple and so easy. This guy's vision and reading of the game were unbelievable. We won 1-0. I came home with my England shirt and my wife took one look at it and said, "It's dry. Are you sure you played?!" She was so used to me being wet through with sweat.

UNDER MCGARRY FOR a few years we were top six every season and qualified for Europe. We were a bit short of being real title contenders alongside Liverpool, Derby and Leeds and I think we could have done with a bigger squad to be able to rotate players a bit more. For example, in my heart of hearts I believe I was at Wolves too long. They should have sold me to make some money and allow new blood to come in, but they let players like me, Geoff Palmer and John McAlle get to the end of our careers, so they couldn't get any cash back for us and therefore didn't generate any money out of the squad for most of the 1970s. That's one of the reasons the club got into difficulties financially, let alone giving them the problem of the team getting old together.

By the time I was 23, the Football League brought this ruling in where players had to have medicals before the beginning of the season. Now I classed myself as being one of the fittest players in the club and I enjoyed training, I never had any problems with it, so I had this routine medical and they did this ECG and found an abnormality in my heartbeat. They were worried it could be so serious it might kill me, let alone end my career. I was kept in intensive care in Wolverhampton Hospital for about six weeks, which was horrible for my wife because she had to come in with the kids in tow and see me in the middle of this ward with people dying all around me. It was a terrible time. I was devastated because I had just bought a new house and had two young children. It could have destroyed all that. The club were very supportive. I don't think anyone got close to Bill McGarry, but I think I got as close as anyone. He didn't show his emotions at all, but he made sure that my family were OK. The initial scare passed when they saw I was actually alright and not suffering at all, but then they couldn't work out what the problem was. After six weeks I was released, but even when I got out I wasn't allowed to play.

Eventually, after six months, the club sent me to London to see a specialist and he gave me the all clear. It turned out that I had an irregular heart beat, but that it was normal to me. I believe that is quite common actually, but you wouldn't know unless you had a test. It was a nasty time, particularly for my wife. But I got the all-clear and then had to get fit again. That didn't take long as I wasn't one to put weight on and I looked after myself. As much as anything it was the adrenaline of wanting to get back so much that spurred me on.

WHEN I GOT back into the side we got to the UEFA Cup Final and then won the League Cup two years later. I don't think me coming into the team made all that difference, I'd like to believe it was the case, but I don't think so. It certainly all slotted into place and we did well. I actually think we should have won a lot more around that time. I mean I played in three FA Cup semi-finals, but never got through to the Final. At least we won the League Cup – twice!

I really enjoyed the 1974 Final, but the day passed by so quickly I didn't have time to take it all in. So when it came round again in 1980 I relished every minute. We had a good team under the enthusiastic John Barnwell. A lot of the stalwarts from McGarry's team were still together such as John McAlle, Geoff Palmer and Kenny Hibbitt.

Then John Barnwell pulled off a fantastic deal. We'd only just survived a bit of a relegation battle the season before and in September 1979 he sold Steve Daley to Manchester City for around £1.5m, which was a phenomenal amount of money.

Then he brought in Andy Gray and Emlyn Hughes. Andy was the new club record signing at just under £1.5m, I think. At the other end of the scale Emlyn only cost about £90,000.

It really was just those couple of changes, bringing in Andy and Emlyn, that made all the difference. It just clicked then. Emlyn was a brilliant buy for the club. He'd won everything at Liverpool apart from the League Cup and had only recently lifted the European Cup. Then he comes to us and in his first season wins the League Cup, the only cup he didn't win at Liverpool. We'd won nothing. Some had won the 1974 League Cup, but most hadn't won a thing. Emlyn had a great career, but just because he played for Liverpool didn't give him the divine right to win things, it was because he put the effort in. He'd been one of the all-time greats at Anfield and he brought all that effervescence and enthusiasm for the game to Wolves and it spilled out on to other people. He also had that winning mentality. I remember the times I've played against Liverpool. Anfield was *the* place you really wanted to play. In all my 15 years at Wolves I don't think we ever won there. I remember the first time we played them up there and at half-time I was even more drenched with sweat than normal. As we jogged off I even counted how many players they'd got because I couldn't believe the way they played, because you'd get past one and then there'd be another and another. They had endless energy and the way they zipped the ball about was brilliantl. What a team.

Both these new signings were vital to our progress. Suddenly, from being relegation fodder we were in two semi-finals and finished in the top six on the back of a tremendous season.

We felt that year we were a good cup team as we were very hard to beat. Some teams are just like that. The year we beat Forest we had a lot of clean sheets on the run in the cups and for us to stop Forest scoring in the final was a feat in itself. They'd won the previous two League Cup competitions and had beaten Liverpool in the semi-final and a few weeks later Forest were winning the European Cup – again, for the second time in a row!

I would give a lot of credit to Mel Eves and Kenny Hibbitt who did a brilliant job up and down the line. It's a soul destroying job, I think, but we had these two workhorses who put in such a lot of effort. It's amazing to think a player of Kenny's ability wasn't playing in the middle, but he did so well out on the wing.

Defensively we had a settled back four. We worked well as I'd played with Geoff Palmer for years and it was easy enough to play with Emlyn. I think George came in for the final because John McAlle broke his leg in the semi-final. George did a good job. He had a big heart and it didn't matter how he played, he wanted the ball and he wanted to keep playing. Sometimes people hide and their heads drop when it doesn't go well for them, but George would keep asking for the ball. John McAlle was a fantastic tackler and was unfortunate to miss the game, but it gave George his Wembley chance.

OUR RUN TO the final was quite tough, starting at Burnley, and then we faced a test at Crystal Palace. We were 1-0 down at half-time and then Hibbitt and Eves scored the two goals to give us the win. There were big crowds for the League Cup around that time. Some of the Molineux crowds topped 30,000 during the run. Maybe they could sense, as we did, that we had something good going on and that we could possibly get close to winning something that year.

Next we drew at QPR and won at home and in the quarter-final we drew Grimsby, who were near the top of the Third Division at the time. The games just seemed to keep ending level. Eventually we won in a second replay, 2-0 at their ground.

Then in the semi-final we drew another lower division side, which sounds great on paper, but you're always worried about slipping up – especially this close to Wembley. This time it was Swindon, who'd had a great run to get this far, knocking out First Division sides Stoke and Arsenal. It's always tricky for top level clubs to play lower division sides in the cups. You could play them and beat them nine times out of ten, but on the one occasion you could let your standards drop and that's when upsets happen. John Barnwell always used to say, "You've got to match these for graft and effort for 90 minutes. And then our extra class will tell and we'll score the goal that matters." You do have to match them for effort

I don't remember much about those games, but I do remember losing away from home 2-1 and that was a particularly tough game and obviously not a great result. But we took them home and beat them 3-1 to complete the aggregate win. We were in a really good run of form in February, when we won through to the final. It's confidence really. You get such a lift from getting to Wembley. We beat Liverpool, Norwich and Manchester United (at Old Trafford) that month. Once people start winning they get used to it, they like it. It becomes a habit. John Barnwell always used to say, "We've got to string four or five results together."

ONCE YOU'RE THROUGH to Wembley there's all sorts of stuff that comes along. I think we did a song. It was a laugh, as we weren't bloody singers, that's for sure. The town was buzzing as Wolves hadn't really had a lot to cheer about since the 1950s. Suddenly all the chat was about us. For the second time in six years.

I'm not superstitious. A lot of players are. They don't get up until a certain time, they put their socks on the same way. Kenny Hibbitt was a bit superstitious. He used to wear the same suit if we won. He would then wear it until we lost. So as you can imagine, he had a few suits! The build up wasn't anything different to the norm except we travelled down to London on the Thursday night, but we tried to keep it low key and the same as any week to not get us too nervous or over-hyped.

One of the great things at Wembley is coming up that tunnel and we were lucky as the Wolves supporters were at the opposite end to the tunnel so they could see us coming out and it was a deafening racket and wonderful sight. The atmosphere was breathtaking. This Gold and Black was wonderful. The hairs on the back of your neck are up as you enter the stadium which you've dreamt of as a kid. I think every footballer should be able to play there at least once in his career, because it is something else. Oh, it really was. The first time we played at Wembley it passed me by. We'd won and I enjoyed everything about it, but it left like a dream really; but the second time I could take it all in a lot more.

FOREST WERE EUROPEAN champions and were expected to win, but we didn't try anything new for them. We just stuck to our system. John had this idea of two wide players who dropped into midfield and that restricted Forest's movement a lot, it made the game narrower. It helped us full-backs and restricted their wingers like John Robertson. As underdogs we always thought we had a chance. I mean around that time Sunderland had beaten Leeds and then just afterwards West Ham beat Arsenal in FA Cup Finals. When it comes down to it, what matters is who wants it most on the day. Back in 1974 I'd known all along it was our day. I wasn't 100 per cent sure this time, but I fancied our chances.

Cloughie was awesome really. He was like a god. You have to respect a guy like him because of what he'd done in football. Forest were a great team. They weren't outstanding individuals, but he blended a team of good players who would put the work in. I marked Trevor Francis. He was a good player, but on the day everything went for us. As the game went on it seemed like it was our day. They began to get frustrated at the lack of space they had as I think they'd looked forward to playing expansively on that big Wembley pitch. Well we stopped them doing that. The game can't have been much to watch, but we knew what we were doing. Just biding our time.

And, contrary to popular belief we did create some chances. John Richards and Willie Carr got the ball in the net from close range once. But referees are very protective. The goalkeeper only had to put his hand up and it was a free kick.

BUT THEN CAME the goal. This long, no-hope ball really, from Peter Daniel at the back and then you've got Peter Shilton, one of the best goalkeepers in the world, coming out to pick it up. But Forest had one change to their usual line-up. Dave Needham was playing in central defence in place of the suspended Larry Lloyd and he and Shilton got mixed up. It was a terrible mess and they fell over each other. I don't know what went on, but the look on Andy Gray's face was worth it all. He couldn't believe it. That was probably the easiest goal he'd ever scored.

It was odd for me as I was so far away from the goal when Andy scored. He ran off behind the goal and I was so far away from him I thought "I'm not going to chase him!" We all celebrated in our own way when the ball went in. But I had to think straight way. Right, they're going to kick off here and Francis is going to get the ball. So I couldn't dwell on the goal too much. But I think Forest did. It affected them. They came at us, though, and gave us a tough time defensively.

I do think that the goal probably wouldn't have happened if Larry Lloyd had been playing. He was the sort of player to just get rid of the ball without asking any questions. He would just head it out and then try to sort things out, so it probably was some sort of communication problem between Shilton and Needham that brought the whole thing about. They just got mixed up; a misunderstanding. But that's football.

After that I just couldn't see them getting a goal back. In the heat of a Wembley final to go ahead gives you so much confidence. It lifts you and makes you play even harder. We were ahead and determined to keep hold of the lead, but they put plenty of pressure on us towards the end.

Then the final whistle and we'd won. It's a magnificent moment. I mean if you ask anyone in this book about winning cups they'll all tell you about how much adrenaline is pumping round your body. You don't want it to end. To win it is a wonderful feeling and you want to stay on that high as long as possible. You feel so elated. You want to stay there and keep parading the cup around Wembley. God knows what it's like to lose there.

It's just like a dream to win and it takes you ages to come down. Especially after all the build-up and anxiety leading up to it. That night my legs were twitching and my body was twitching when I climbed into bed. But that's what you play for. You play to win games and trophies.

I ONLY VAGUELY remember collecting my medal. All I was really interested in was finding my family. My two kids were made up as they'd been too small when we'd won it in 1974. I was busy looking for them in the stands and when I found them that was my special time. It was a great day for them. When you're a professional footballer your children attend schools where not all the kids are Wolves supporters and even when they are they sometimes give the kids some stick and I remember my daughter saying, "I can't wait to go to school on Monday, Dad". And I hadn't appreciated how much stick she'd had. I think she revelled in that victory as much as me! Kids can be cruel can't they and she was having her moment of glory.

It was different to win the cup on this occasion as we'd scored two goals against City in 1974 and played well, but this was just the one, rather fluky goal. But that doesn't matter when it comes down to it. You ask all the Wolves supporters who won the League Cup in 1980 and it is there in black and white in the record books. Doesn't matter that we didn't play that well or that Forest had much more of the ball. The result stands and that's all that matters in cup football.

The Doog used to make me laugh because he'd score goals that he'd meant to belt, but they trickled in and he'd take some stick from the lads and he would always say, "Read the papers tomorrow". It was always his name in black and white recording the goal he scored, not the fact that it went in off the back of his head or his backside! It doesn't matter how you score.

HAVING WON THE League Cup we suddenly found ourselves playing against PSV Eindhoven in the UEFA Cup. There was a lot of controversy surrounding the tie. I had a calf injury and it was 50/50 as to whether I played. I had to come off with it in the away leg in the end and so can't remember much about it. They had a dodgy penalty in a 3-1 win at their place and then we could only win 1-0 in the return, so we went out 3-2 on aggregate. That seemed to be the end of a pretty decent Wolves side. In fact I was lucky to get out before it all exploded.

When I was at Huddersfield the coach was Ian Greaves, the former Manchester United full-back and later on he came to Wolves. I remember him coming in one day when I was recovering from injury. I was 34 then and knew my time was up soon. What I didn't know was that the club were going under and Ian came to me and said, "I think you should go and talk to Richie Barker at Stoke."

That very night Richie Barker came to our house outside Stafford and I agreed to sign. He told me about all the players he was buying: Mark Chamberlain, Dave Watson, Mickey Thomas, Sammy McIlroy. I went back to playing right-back and Chambo could have put five years on my career. He was such a fast winger. It worked and we did very well in the 1982/83 season.

When I first moved to Stoke it was the end of the 1981/82 season and there were about ten games left. Stoke were hovering just above the relegation zone and Wolves were right down in it. And about my third or fourth game for Stoke was against Wolves. I didn't want to play, but I had to. That's what happens in professional football. Wolves went one up at half-time, but it was a tight game and fairly tough. Then Andy Gray got sent off and Stoke won 2-1. From there City stayed up and the Wolves just went down and down and down to the Fourth Division and it was really sad. Had they won that game the roles would have been reversed. I couldn't believe it. I couldn't bear to see what happened to them during the Eighties. Thankfully it's all changed now.

I SAID I wasn't superstitious, I had my routine rather than a superstition. When I finished playing it stayed with me as I'd been doing the same things on a Saturday morning for around 20 years. In fact I still got the adrenaline rush in the morning for about six years after I'd retired and I needed to get out and go for a run to get rid of the frustration and the energy I had. You don't realise until you finish how much it all stays with you. I couldn't get it out of my head. In fact there's still not a day goes by that I don't think about it. They were wonderful years.

STEVE BULL: BORN 28 MARCH 1965, TIPTON; 561 GAMES, 306 GOALS

# Steve Bull MBE

## Wolves 1 Nottingham Forest 1

## League Cup Final

## Saturday 15 March 1980

I WAS ALWAYS a striker. Always a goalscorer. That's it. I'll run up there, give me the ball and I'll score you a goal.

When you're young, all boys want to play football. I just wanted to play. It didn't matter about professionally. They put me in goal at school because I was too selfish and wouldn't pass the ball. And then I was too small to be any good, so they put me on the bench. And every time I come on I got the ball and I wouldn't pass to anyone until I scored. They were all shouting "pass it here" and all I wanted to do was score a goal. Eventually I got into the school team and started playing regularly and scoring and I got scouted by Tipton Town, my local non-league side in the Banks' Brewery League. I was only 16 at the time and all the lads in the team were 19, 20, even 30, you know. All well old, so I was like a little dot in a giant's den. I got on the bench every now and again and I'd come on for ten minutes here, 15 minutes there and get kicked about by these big lads I was playing against. Later on that stood me in good stead because when it happened in the Football League I'd been put through the mill by my experience at Tipton and I knew how to deal with all the kicking I got. So I played for them on a Saturday afternoon and then for Newy Goodman on a Sunday morning. I won quite a few cups with them on a Sunday in the local leagues.

Come 19 and I'm working 12-hour days stacking shelves at Dom Holdings, getting customers' orders together for all the building supplies they had there. I was scouted down to the Albion by a guy called Sid Day. He said to me, "I've had a word with the manager John Giles and he wants you to have a trial. Every Tuesday night and Thursday night the under-14s play…" And I thought "I've got to go from men's football with Tipton to go and play with kids?!" So I said "Well, I'll try it." So every Tuesday night and Thursday night I was down the Albion training. When I started I thought to myself "I'm going to rip these to pieces" and I couldn't believe it. They were dribbling me all over the place. Under-14s. Dribbling *me* all over the place. I was 19! "Little gits," I thought. I gradually got into it and began to play intermediate games for Albion on a Saturday morning. So then I was working a 60-hour week, playing on Saturday mornings, Saturday afternoons and Sunday mornings. Plus training during the evenings. So it began to take its toll. In fact I can feel my knees now because of all games I played over the years.

But it worked. Eventually, because I was scoring goals for fun, they offered me a three-month trial. I had been scoring plenty of goals in the lower teams, but now I was tested in the reserves. I scored goals there too. No worries at all. Eventually they offered me a one-year deal. Nobby Stiles (Assistant Manager) discussed it with me and he said, "What are you on at work at the moment, Steve?" I was actually working through an agency and earning a good whack, £27 per day I think, but Albion were only offering £100 a week. So I asked Nobby what I should do. He told me to take the chance, so I took the gamble of signing for 12 months and knocked all the work on the head, because Nobby said to me, "When you're at work it takes a lot out of you. You need to rest." And

I stopped playing all me other football as well. Nobby told me, "We would like to see you in full time training." That was 1984.

And he was right. I just blossomed then. I scored even more goals and then, finally, got my chance to play in the first team, against Ipswich Town. We lost 4-3 but I scored two goals. When I scored the second one the supporters all started going ape. And I thought "What's going on here?" I thought "I like this. I love it. I love it. This is an easy job this is" and Albion were in the First Division at the time. A massive club. The strikers at that time were Imre Varadi, Garth Crooks and George Riley. All experienced players and they were on a fair bit of money as opposed to my pittance. But I couldn't see no reason why I couldn't hold down a place in the team.

Not long after that game Ron Saunders called me off the training ground. He said, "Steve. Somebody's come in for you." I says, "Who?" And he said, "Halifax." Dead pan just like that. I had no idea who they were, where they came from or anything. Then he says, "No, no. Don't worry. It's Wolves. They've come in for you and Andy Thompson." So I asked him, "Ron, what's my future here?" And he replied, "Well, I don't think you've got a first touch for this division." His exact words. And I went, "Do I need to go then?" And he said, "It'll be in your best interests to go." I knew then that he didn't want me. That's why it gets my goat when I get these Albion supporters coming up to me saying, "Why did you leave?" Because I didn't leave. They sold me.

And I also want to get down on paper right now the fact that I am a Liverpool fan. Not Wolves, not Albion. At the time, late Seventies and early Eighties, they were winning everything in sight and were on the telly every time. That's why I supported them. You ask kids now and they'll say Man U, Chelsea and Arsenal, because they are always on the telly.

Ian Rush was always my favourite in that great team. I liked David Fairclough too. Every time he came off the bench I thought, "He's going to score." And he did. He was known as super sub.

SO ME AND Andy Thompson drove down to the ground the same afternoon; him with his moustache and me with my leather jacket. We were like Starsky and Hutch down the M5. We thought, "We're having this, like." When we got there we found this dilapidated old ground. We took one look at it and thought "Jesus Christ." The door nearly fell off its hinges when we came in. Clare Peters, who still works for the club, saw us in and told us to sit down. There actually only were two chairs in the whole place. I thought, "What are we doing?" Thommo said, "Let's see what they offer before making any decisions, eh." So they had us in to see Graham Turner, the manager. He totally sold the club to us, telling us all about their plans, the new ground and saying, "You could be a big part of this if you come here. I want you to come and score goals and I'll guarantee you first team football." Within six minutes the deal was done. I think he put me on about £150 a week and a £4,500 signing-on fee and in 1986 that was a lot of money. I thought "Great. I can get a car with that." If I knew then what I know now, I'd have put all of that £4,500 on me scoring 300 goals for this club. I'd have got 100-1 at least! I'd have been a millionaire then.

Graham Turner was a good manager. In fact if you ask me, "Who is the best manager you played under?" it would be him, with the possible exception of Bobby Robson with England. Graham is a great man-manager. He did as much as anybody to get this club back up the leagues and out of the mess it was in. Him, not me. Because he actually built the side.

Mind you it didn't start that well. The first game me and Thommo went to was away at Chorley. That was at Burnden Park, Bolton's ground and Wolves lost 3-0 in the FA Cup. That was just about the lowest of the low. I didn't even know what league they were in. Wolves were third from bottom of the Fourth Division at the time. The club was ready to go into liquidation. We thought, "Oh my God. What have we done, signing for these?"

I hadn't considered there being any problem if the club had folded. I thought that if I didn't succeed here then I'd go and get a job. That was my attitude then. Because I'm a worker. But thankfully it just took off. Within a few weeks we had totally revamped the side. Some of the existing players stayed. We had Mark Kendall in goal, Floyd Street at centre-half and Andy Mutch up front. But certain players came in like Nigel Vaughan in midfield, Robbie Dennison and Keith Downing. It felt like a side then. That carried us all the way through the rest of the season and we had a great run only losing three games after 1st January 1987. We managed to make the play-offs, but just lost to Aldershot. The next year we went up and then we won the Third Division at the first time of asking.

The gaffer always knew what I liked. He'd tell players to knock the ball over the top and I'd get after it and try and score a goal. I was just direct. I was an old fashioned centre-forward. Me and Andy Mutch really hit it off too. He would hold it up for me to come up and have a shot. We complemented each other so well. I was from Tipton and he was a Scouser and we didn't really know what we were saying to each other, but we knew where each other was going to be. He would say, "Eh. Calm down, calm down." And I'd be like, "What are you saying?!" He had a great left foot and a cracking penalty taker. He got over 50 penalties for us. He was a little dwarf really, but he had a massive, massive ability to run. He had these little legs. In fact around Christmas we had this thing where we told him he couldn't come into training because he had to go and star in the local *Snow White and the Seven Dwarves*! I still think to this day that he left a year early. I know he fell out with the manager, but I still think if he'd stayed we'd have had a good chance to go up again.

THAT WAS THE best spirit of any Wolves side I played in. Because everyone was just about on the same money, we all dug in for each other. But when you got the big money boys coming in later on, you got all this "you shouldn't be on that" and "I'm worth this." You deserve what you're earning. That's my motto.

We always used to have the Tuesday club after training. We used to leg it all day on a Tuesday and I mean run. Leg it. All the way up the stands and around the pitch. For a good hour and a half. The gaffer would say, "Go and enjoy the afternoon off now." We had Wednesday off, so we could go out together on a Tuesday evening. The social thing was superb. Absolutely superb. No matter what was going on every player would be there. Nowadays you won't get that. We had to be in bright as a button on Thursday, mind. There wasn't really a leader as such. In latter years Ally Robertson was the club captain and he'd say, "OK. We're all off to the Odd Spot in Birmingham and we're going to have a few drinks." So we all went together. No worries.

Ally was a good captain, a good leader. We didn't concede many with him and Floyd and Gary at the back. Being ex-Albion I didn't think the Wolves fans would take to him. But they saw how committed he was and they loved him. I never had a problem with people and the Wolves v Albion thing. I think it would be best if both sides were doing really well and the rest of the Midlands clubs too and then there'd be derbies every week. I had some banter with people, but it was never an issue. In fact I've never had an argument with one Wolves fan. I respect them and they respect me, I think. Once I'd scored my first goal they got behind me and it helped that the crowds started coming back. I think my first game there only 3,500 here. Eventually we had 25,000. And when that old South Stand was full with 9,000 people, back then when it was just steps going up into the distance with a big roof on, if you scored in front of that you knew about it because it was echoey. It was different class.

We had a joker in our squad called David Barnes, a full back. He was a good laugh. And then Mark Kendall. He was a character. Like a laughing policeman - which is funny because he is a policeman now. He was a good keeper in his time. He was agile and had the gift of the gab. Then there was Tom Bennett. He was Jack the lad. He strutted about the place thinking "I'm here. I'm gorgeous." Mark Venus had got the hardest left foot side-foot I've ever seen. Like we would hit with the laces, he could hit it with the inside of his foot just as hard. Pinged it. Woosh! He could talk as well. He thought he knew more about football than anybody else, though. He can't pick horses, mind. A rubbish tipster!

Robbie Dennison, was a jinky winger. Two or three tricks and then the ball was in the box. Sometimes these days you see wingers trying too many tricks as they go down the wing and they end up having to pass the ball back to the full-back. Denno would get it in early so that I knew when it was coming in and could be in there ready. He scored some great free kicks as well.

Keith Downing was like a little Jack Russell biting at everyone's ankles to win the ball. But he had to be with Cooky around, because Cooky would stray off all over the place looking for the ball. He had an amazing engine. Iron lungs. He could run all day. He didn't know where he was running, but he could keep going. And he could pick me out all day with different kinds of passes. To feet, over the top; he was fantastic. I would say 40 per cent of my goals were off Cooky's left foot putting me in.

Our squad was very together, so when we got into the First Division we loved it. We'd come up straight through the lower divisions. It was a big leap, but we'd got the team to adjust and Graham was getting a bit more money to put into the side. He had an eye for talent as well. He added Paul Cook into the team and his passes opened up defences. We'd blown teams away a lot of the time in the previous seasons simply by our power and presence. In the First Division it was tougher because it was a battle. Some players were coming up to a level that some of them probably were outstaying their welcome, but they were still proud and battled on. I've always said that you need to battle to get out of this division and then change to a passing style to play in the Premiership, Division One whatever it's called. You saw it in 2005 when West Ham were the best footballing side in the First Division, but they struggled to make the play-offs, When they got into the Premiership they did alright.

Route one normally works at this level and below. Why have ten or 15 passes when you score goals quicker that way. In fact I'd scored nine goals in seven games in the autumn of 1989, but I got injured then and I was just getting back into my stride around Christmas. I scored on Boxing Day at Hull, but we lost 3-1 there. We'd gone down to about 11th in the table, after looking like we could be there or thereabouts for the play-offs despite only just having come up. So we needed something just to give us a bit of a kickstart again.

THIS GAME WAS special to me because I was on the brink of going to the Word Cup in 1990. It was New Year's Eve and we'd travelled up on the coach to Tyneside. Obviously everyone else is partying that night, but footballers can't because they've got to play the next day. There were loads of parties in the hotel and we were eating our pasta and steaks. We'd had a training session and the gaffer come in and said, "By the way lads, it's New Year's Eve and I want you in bed by 12 o'clock. But you can have a couple of halves." He knew that we were OK to have a drink and we wouldn't take the mickey. But for some reason that night we were on one. There were four of us left after about 11 o'clock. Me, Thommo, Cooky and Mutchy. That was a good combination of the four of us. And about seven glasses of wine later we were still up. We phoned our wives after midnight to say "love you loads" or whatever. And then we still kept going. I was thinking, "What are we doing?" And we sat there and said, "Shall we have another glass for the road?" Remember we'd got to play Newcastle the next day. We were already half cut, all four of us. "Yeah, we'll be alright, we'll be OK" we said, because you're invincible once you've had a few, aren't you? By then we were thinking "tomorrow will be easy. We'll beat them, no worries at all!"

I don't know what time we got to sleep. I don't think it was too late actually. The next morning the gaffer got us into the team meeting and all four of us looked like death warmed up. We were just sitting there dazed. We got away with that one. We had to just get on with even though we still felt crap.

So we got to St James' Park. It was freezing cold and there must have been about 2,500 Wolves fans who'd all chartered airplanes to come up to see us play. They'd all got antlers on, snowmen outfits, reindeers, Santa hats, all cheering for us - and then it kicks in to you. What did we do last night?! These have spent all their hard-earned money for us to have a drink and play shit. And I thought to myself, "I'm never doing that again."

NEWCASTLE HAD MADE a big signing just before that game, an experienced midfielder called Roy Aitken from Celtic and this was going to be his debut, so we knew that he would be on the go from the start. He was a good player. Big and strong. He liked to put his foot in to the tackle. They also had Micky Quinn who'd banged a few goals in that season. Floyd and Gary Bellamy were due to keep him quiet. I think Floyd went on him because Gary wasn't exactly the fastest. His strength was in the air. Floyd was a determined bloke and if he got a bee in his bonnet he made sure he did his job and kept his man quiet. So if I'd been Quinny that day I would have given up and gone out on the wing or something. Floyd kept him totally quiet and that was his job. Just as it was mine to score goals.

It was 0-0 in the first half and we were kicking towards their fans. They were the better side, not surprisingly. Mark McGhee played up front for them and he missed an absolute sitter. If our fans knew then that he'd end up as manager here they'd have given him more stick wouldn't they? But he missed a sitter in the first half and the gaffer said, "That's OK. I can live with that. I think we can snatch this. If we can come away from here with a 1-0 or a draw I'll be very happy with the performance." We were thinking "Jesus Christ. If he knew what we'd done he'd kill us!"

So we got out there for the second half and I couldn't believe the way it happened. For the first goal, the ball come to Paul Cook on the left hand side. He drilled it into the near post where I was running in. It was so hard I thought that it was just going to hit me, so I decided not to actually shoot, but just to let it bounce off the bottom of my foot at speed and it went in the corner. The ball knocked me over it was that hard, so I got up and I was thinking, "I'll have this. The gaffer was right. We are going to win this 1-0." So I was giving it everything in front of our fans with a load of Santas dancing up and down with me.

We wanted to just keep it tight at the back then, to keep them out and hang on to the 1-0. But they didn't really put us under any pressure at all. The second goal came along then. Robbie Dennison had the ball in the middle of the park. He played it forward to Keith Downing, who was in front of him. He let it run through his legs and I ran behind him on to the ball. I went past the keeper and slotted it in with my left foot. 2-0. I was bowled over. And I was in front of the fans again. "Have some of that," I thought. I think Newcastle dipped then. Heads went down.

The third one came along from a corner. It came over and their defender jumped up and it flicked off him to the back post, where I was waiting. Bang. Header. Goal. I was there then. Aeroplane. Hat-trick. You always take a quick look at the linesman to check it's not offside and you're making a fool of yourself. The fans were giving it "Bully, Bully!" I thought "This is class this is. Even though I've had a drink I've scored three against Newcastle!"

And when the fourth went in I thought, "That's taking the mickey. That is taking the mickey." That goal came from Robbie Dennison coming down the middle again. I went out to the right hand side and he played me in. I went round the defender, beat the keeper and poked it in. I can't remember how I celebrated then. It was that mental. It just topped it off. There were always certain teams I could score two or three times against - Port Vale, Leicester, Preston. I don't know why I just could do it. But no way did I ever think I'd score four against Newcastle. Never. I got on the coach afterwards and I just had an orange juice to celebrate. I figured I'd had my booze for the occasion! So orange juice and that's it. But all the players were saying to me after that I should do it more often. It wasn't the first time I'd scored four, mind you. I'd done that already against Preston in a 6-0 win and then I got another four against Vale a couple of weeks later. I can't really remember them though. Its funny how this one stands out amongst the New Year celebrations and then going to the World Cup in Italy, which was unbelievable. 1990 was a brilliant year.

That was definitely the first time and the last time the players ever had a drink like that before a game as far as I know. But for the Newcastle players to play like that and let us score four goals. Maybe it should have been them that went out drinking that night instead of us!